Behind the View

Behind the View

Life and times in Cressbrook -
a Derbyshire mill village

Behind the View was written by the people of Cressbrook and was supported by the Local Heritage Initiative - a partnership between the Heritage Lottery Fund, Nationwide Building Society and the Countryside Agency.
The project was managed by Carole Perks, Chris Gilbert and Hilary Stephens between October 2003 and September 2005.

Published by Carole Perks, Chris Gilbert and Hilary Stephens in 2005

The moral rights of the authors has been asserted.

ISBN 0-9551750-0-3

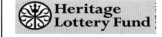  

Acknowledgements

Carole, Chris and Hilary would like to thank the following people with apologies if we've forgotten anyone.

Jean Rider and the Local Heritage Initiative for their help, support and funding.

The people of Cressbrook who made a direct contribution to the creation of the book as authors of pieces:
Gareth and Jan Watkins, Dave and Ann Archer, Beryl Hull-Bailey, Pat Kelly, Max and Alice Savage, Connor Longson, Jean Stone, Chris Gilbert, Hilary and Helena Stephens, Carole Perks.

The people of Cressbrook who made a direct contribution to the creation of the book as interviewers in the Oral History project:
Roz Savage, Jane Money, Marie Howes, Wendy Morrison, Jill Turner, Sophie Godber, Carole Perks, Hilary Stephens and Chris Gilbert.

The people of Cressbrook, past and present, who patiently submitted to the Oral History project:
Ken and Vera Munns, Miriam and Gordon Sharpley, Arthur Barnes, Paul Dickie, Dorothy Mycock, Harriet Allen, Aubrey and Elisabeth Howe, Isobel Sutcliffe, Carol Harland, Gary Pitchford, Brian Bingham, Derek Cooke, Marjorie Hoyle, Mavis and David Holmes.

The people and friends of Cressbrook who enthusiastically shared records of their lives and their experiences with us:
Lynne Hoare, Pat Longson, Joan Beresford, Ron and Una Hill, Malcolm and Maureen Burton, Maureen Allen, Jo Hoare, Julia Prigg, Beryl Hull-Bailey, Tony Hill, Gordon Bowering, Jim Grindley, Mick Daulton.

Cressbrook Community Group and Cressbrook Club

Other individuals and groups who have very generously given us advice, lent or given us access to their materials and donated their own time towards research at our request:
Lillias Bendall, Frank Galbraith, Joe Dugdale of the Derbyshire Rural Community Council
Amanda Searle of the LHI
Catherine Mate and Carol Ribbon of the Peak District National Park
Ray Manley of the Peak District National Park
Mr Nicholas Davie-Thornhill of the Stanton Estate Company
Mr Roger Hoare of Brooke-Taylor and Company on behalf of The Bingham Trust
Mr Kevin Bolton of the Manchester Archives
Derbyshire Records Office in Matlock
Bakewell Library
Ben Lebas and Debbie Worral of English Nature, Bakewell
Nick Tomlinson, Project Manager, Picture The Past, Heanor Library
Alyson Rogers at English Heritage
Colin Hyde of East Midlands Oral History Association
Philip Gibb, NT Gibbs,(Tideswell butchers).

Photographs:
The people and friends of Cressbrook who searched out old photographs in cupboards, lofts and long-forgotten photo albums. Also, new photographs by Paul Radcliffe, Chris Gilbert and Roz Savage.

Illustrations:
Keith Hislop, Chris Gilbert and Jeff Perks.

Design and Production:
Carole Perks.

For Services Rendered:
Margaret Wood, South Yorkshire Transcription Services.
Sandra Hogben, editorial advice.
Printed by B & B Press Limited, Rotherham, South Yorkshire on Satimat Art which has the following environmental qualities - ECF, acid free, recyclable and biodegradable. This material is sourced from sustainable and managed forests.

Contents

Matthew Dickie's water turbine, restored in 2003 by David Holmes

7   FOREWORD

8   CHAPTER 1 1765-1792
     A most picturesque situation

12   CHAPTER 2 1792-1835
     Dark satanic mills?

20   CHAPTER 3 1835-1893
     Self-interested charity

30   CHAPTER 4 1893-1965
     Life in a model village
34   Remember when....
        Gordon and Miriam Sharpley,
        Vera Munns, Pat Kelly, Isobel
        Sutcliffe, Brian Bingham,
        Marjorie Hoyle
42   Two lives
        Arthur Barnes and Paul Dickie
48   The mill process in 1946
50   The mill clock & gas house
        Isobel Sutcliffe and Arthur Barnes
52   Religion in Cressbrook

54   A railroad through the valley
58   On track
        Ken Munns
60   End of term report
        Gordon and Miriam Sharpley,
        Vera Munns, Isobel Sutcliffe ,
        Marjorie Hoyle
68   Taking the register
        Mrs Daykin
72   Our evacuee
        Pat Kelly
74   A farmers wife
        Harriet Allen

78   CHAPTER 5
     End of an era
84   Cat flaps and other things
        Derek Cooke
86   Trinity House
        Jan and Gareth Watkins
        Dave and Ann Archer
89   Cressbrook Hall
        Beryl Hull-Bailey
92   Cressbrook Band

94   In tune
        Ken Munns and Brian Bingham
98   A farmers boy
        Aubrey Howe
102 Born 'n bred
        Carol Harland

106 CHAPTER 6
     Life in Cressbrook

116 CHAPTER 7
     Thoroughly modern mill

118 CHAPTER 8
     Flora and Fauna and Tourists
122 A Winters Tale
        Mrs Daykin, Aubrey Howe,
        Harriet Allen
124 Websites and book references

Foreword

*B*ehind the View is the story of Cressbrook as told by the people who live there. It is a living account of this special place, charting its evolution from its industrial origins to the present day. The project started in 2003 as the brainchild of Carole Perks who, together with Hilary Stephens and Chris Gilbert secured a grant from the Local Heritage Initiative, a Countryside Agency project, for funding of the major part of the costs of the book. The conditions for the grant included the involvement of members of the community in the book's creation and over the next two years Carole, Hilary and Chris organised and cajoled residents into full contribution to the project, leading to the book you are now reading.

There has been significant interest in the history of Cressbrook for some years. In 1959, before Cressbrook Mill went bankrupt for the final time, the Department of the Environment (later to become English Heritage) earmarked it for conservation and catalogued it photographically. There have also been a number of previous formal attempts to document its history.

The most notable publication being the papers written by Margaret Mackenzie for the *Derbyshire Archeological Journal* in 1970 wherein she described the earliest years of the site up until its purchase in 1835 by McConnel and Company. There have also been informal records made by people within the village who have come to love the place and felt compelled to document what they found here. In the 1960s the role of local historian fell to Edward Sheldon and much of the material he was able to gather through word of mouth at that time was subsequently borne out by Margaret Mackenzie's work. The first consolidated account of the village and its history was the paperback *Cressbrook*, published in 1996 and written by Maureen Allen, who was born in the village at Home Farm.

External agencies in the form of the Peak District National Park, English Heritage and English Nature have also been very much aware of the importance of the site and have maintained their own records but **Behind the View** is the most ambitious attempt to date to pull together a complete history of Cressbrook. It exploits all of the known sources of information about the village and presents for the first time an account of the hitherto scantily-researched period after 1835, where Margaret Mackenzie's work ends.

This project is also particularly notable for its valuable and revealing oral history component. Unique and original research records formally and at first-hand accounts of the changes experienced by this small community by the people who have lived here. In doing so, the project has preserved these experiences both forever and in their own words.

Carole, Chris and Hilary
taking advantage of
Solly's seat

Aerial view of Cressbrook

> " ...On rising the hill beyond it
> (in the road to Tideswell) a
> wall guards a precipice on
> the left, from whence is a
> most enchanting scene. The bottom is a
> narrow dale, called Monsall Dale,
> running between the mountains on your
> left hand, and, opposite to the place
> where you stand, winding round the
> corner of a projecting hill, and at length
> lost behind another, which seems to close
> the vale. It is watered by the lively little
> river Wye, which rising near Buxton,
> about 10 miles off, finds its way between
> the hills and runs through this dale, by
> Ashford, Bakewell, and Haddon Hall,
> into the Derwent.
>
> If you have an inclination to go up this
> dale, and trace the stream towards its
> source, you come to a point of land,
> where the Wye receives another little
> stream, which rises on Wardlow Moor;
> on this last stream is a place called bright
> pool, to which people sometimes go to
> bathe, though it is nothing more than a
> rivulet deeper than the rest; but the
> water of it is supposed to possess some
> medicinal qualities. Higher up is a small
> fall of the current over the rock, not
> worth the trouble of going through the
> bushes to see. At the point of land above
> mentioned, a gentleman to whom it was
> allotted on an inclosure, has made a large
> plantation of lavender, peppermint, and
> other aromatic herbs, and set up a
> distillery of them. This is called
> Cressbrook Dale, and if the
> wood was properly cleared
> away, I am told that it would
> be a Dove Dale in miniature. "

A most picturesque situation

Before the industrial events which changed the valley forever, William Bray visited Monsal and Cressbrook Dales in 1778 and was overwhelmed by what he found

Richard Arkwright

The gentleman distiller to whom William Bray refers in his book *'Sketch of a tour into Derbyshire and Yorkshire'* was one John Baker and the area over which his plantation of aromatic herbs grew was known as Litton Frith[1]. A hosier by trade and originally from the nearby village of Litton, Baker had been granted the land as part of the Enclosures Act of 1764 and lived with his family in a three storey house built into a corner of Water-cum-Jolly[2] Dale, under an overhang that the rock climbing community have since called Rubicon Wall. The sheltered south facing aspect of the land around was clearly most suitable for cultivation because as well as growing aromatic herbs on the Frith, Baker also planted the hillside above his house with

Filbert trees. The floor of the valley immediately in front of the house was Baker's garden, which he called Bee

At Enclosure in 1764

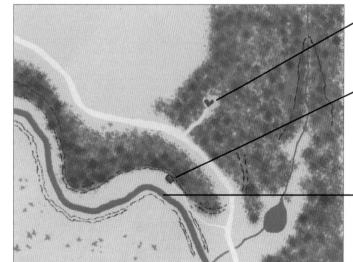

In the woods there are some woodsman's cottages.

John Baker's Rock House is built into the wall of Water-cum-Jolly Dale.

There is little in the area of the Frith. The Wye flows along its bed in the bottom of the gorge and Baker's house is surrounded by his crops.

Stones. The house has long since been demolished but its traces can still be found in the rock wall into which it was set in the form of square seatings, cut to provide purchase for the timbers of the floors and walls of the house. At the time that Bray wrote his piece the waters of the Wye tumbled out of Water-cum-Jolly Dale to the south over an energetic cataract. The potential of the energies carried by swiftly falling waters were being

exploited by the architects of the industrial revolution and a key player in this was Richard Arkwright, who had been experimenting with water-powered cotton spinning since 1768 and already had spinning interests in Nottingham and Derby. Together with Samuel Need and Jebediah Strutt he founded in 1771 the world's first commercially viable water-powered cotton spinning mill at Cromford in Derbyshire. His success at Cromford led to him build more mills and in 1779 his quest for suitable mill sites brought him to Litton Frith and the cataract at Water-cum-Jolly Dale. Records suggest that at this time there were few buildings in the vicinity of Litton Frith and Cressbrook Dale with little else beyond Baker's house other than a couple of lead miner's and woodman's cottages scattered among the trees. Period maps show that the local trackways avoided the area, no doubt because of the inaccessibility caused by the gorges of Water-cum-Jolly and Cressbrook Dale and the steep-sided and heavily forested nature of the enclosing hills. The only access by cart was from Monsal Head, or Headstones as it was then known, to the south, where the Dukes of Devonshire had built a road into the valley to gain access to their farmlands in the valley. They still own those

Artists impression of John Bakers house in Water-cum-Jolly Dale

farmlands today. Arkwright leased from John Baker the southernmost portion of the Frith where it adjoined the gorge at the exit on Water-cum-Jolly. His intention was to harness the power of the Wye in the same manner that he had done with the Derwent at Cromford and at Matlock Bath. He was thwarted in this, however, by an ongoing and bitter dispute with the then Duke of Devonshire who owned the water in the Wye and who barred him from using it at Water-cum-Jolly to power his intended mill. Undeterred, Arkwright turned his attention to the Cress Brook mentioned in Bray's passage. He expanded the bright pool and dammed its exit point, straightened the remainder of the stream's course across the valley floor and employed local craftsman William Newton, previously in the employ if the Duke of Devonshire, to build a wooden cotton-spinning mill at its confluence with the Wye. The precise date of the commencement of this build is obscure, but records suggest that the mill was operating by 1783. After completing the construction of the mill Arkwright engaged Newton as mill manager.

Sir Francis Chantry's sketch of William Newton

Newton was born locally at Cockey Farm near Bretton and although a carpenter and builder by trade, he was also very well read and wrote poetry in his spare time, for which he has subsequently found much greater fame as the so-called 'Minstrel of the Peak' through the patronage of Anna Seward, a society lady from Lichfield.

Newton operated the mill successfully for a few years but it was destroyed by fire on the 15th November 1785. A common occurrence in wooden mills, where the spinning of thread was lit much of the time by candles and oil lamps. The loss of the mill irked Arkwright considerably and evidence suggests that it was not insured. He held Newton to blame for the disaster and promptly sacked him.

Despite the setback Arkwright clearly recognised the potential of the site at Water-cum-Jolly and retained his lease on it. John Baker had died in 1783 and in 1787 Arkwright's son, also called Richard Arkwright, purchased the land outright from John Baker's estate and set about improving the site at Cressbrook. He rebuilt the mill in stone and extended the available accommodation with a row of small cottages to house mill employees. These cottages now no longer exist, having been subsumed by later developments at the mill, but from

About 1810

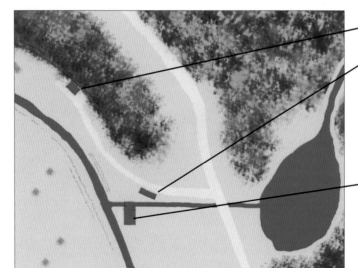

John Bakers Rock House

A row of accomodation cottages houses the small workforce of overseers and managers.

Arkwrights original mill has been rebuilt on the foundations of the first.

Remains of the seatings that supported the floor joists in Rock House can still be seen in Water-cum-Jolly Dale

these humble beginnings the settlement of Cressbrook grew on Litton Frith, at the junction of Cressbrook Dale and Water-cum-Jolly Dale.

Bray's eulogy of Monsal Dale, with its gushing praise for the valley's beauty, was published in 1778 and Arkwright commenced work on the site in 1779. We are fortunate to have a detailed account of the appearance of the valley prior to the events that were to alter its form so radically forever.

1 From 'Fyrhd' - Old English for woodland'

2 From the French 'Jolie', meaning pretty

CRESSBROOK TIME LINE

1763 John Baker, hosier from Litton, is granted the enclosure of Litton Frith. Builds Rock House in Rubicon Wall

1763 France cedes Canada to the British

1778 William Bray visits Monsal Dale and Cressbrook Dale

1779 Richard Arkwright snr leases part of the Frith from John Baker's estate and builds wooden water-powered mill, William Newton hired as mill manager

1783 John Baker dies. His estate is left in some confusion

1785 Fire destroys Mill, Newton sacked

1787 Arkwright jnr builds second mill on foundations of first and buys freehold of Frith from Baker's estate

1789 Storming of the Bastille in Paris

1792 Arkwright snr dies and Samuel Simpson buys mill from Arkwright Jnr

1793 Simpson buys freehold on Frith

1793 Start of the Napoleonic wars

1799 Edmund Baker, John's son, sells Rock House to pay off duties

1809 Mill bankrupt through high taxation due to wars and poor management

1810 Mill and Frith leased by John and Francis Philips at £82 per year. William Newton returns as manager

1812 Napoleon defeated in the Battle of Waterloo

1814 Philips buy Frith freehold from Simpson, negotiates water rights from Devonshires, starts work on Wye/Big Mill, William Newton jnr is resident engineer

1815 End of the Napoleonic conflicts

1816 Wye Mill completed at the cost of £12,000. James Newton, Henry Newton now also engaged in business. Newton

recruits first batch of apprentices from London. Housed in the roof of the mill.

1817 New apprentice house completed

1823 Third mill built. Old Arkwright dam replaced. Apprentice house extended. Newton and family living in Rock House. Cottages in Ravensdale built

1824 John Philips dies. Francis Philips returns to Stockport

1826 Cressbrook Mills put up for sale

1830 William Newton snr dies

1835 Cressbrook Mill purchased by McConnel and Co of Manchester. Henry McConnel begins construction of Cressbrook House

1837 Coronation of Queen Victoria

1838 Cressbrook Mill producing lace thread for Nottingham markets

1840 Henry McConnel plans the building of Lower Wood, Middle Row and Upper Wood cottages

1844 Changes in law prevent all recruitment of apprentices from London

1851 The Great Exhibition opens

1862 Trans-peak railway is opened

1868 Benjamin Disraeli Prime Minister

1871 Henry McConell dies

1874 Upper and Lower Lodges built

1876 General Custer dies at the Battle of the Little Bighorn

1878 Village school is built

1893 Matthew Dickie Jnr Ltd leases Cressbrook and Litton Mills. Cressbrook Mill converted to water turbine

1900 Institute Row is planned and built by Mary Worthington

1901 Death of Queen Victoria

1902 Church of St John the Evangelist built

1904 Mary Worthington dies

1909 Ownership of roads through Cressbrook is transferred to Bakewell Rural Council

1912 Sinking of the Titanic

1914-1918 World War I

1920 Cressbrook Mill converted to steam turbine. Water power.no longer used

1924 Henry Hugo Worthington dies

1925 Cressbrook Mill sold to Matthew Dickie Junior Ltd. William Mallison buys Cressbrook Hall. McConnel's association with the village ends

1931 Primitive Methodist chapel built

1938 Mill bankrupt for the second time.

1939-1945 World War II

1953 Coronation of Queen Elizabeth II

1956 Cressbrook Mill converted to mains electricty

1959 Railway ceases running

1965 Cressbrook Mill ceases all production

1967 Cressbrook Mills listed as Grade I by Department of the Environment

1974 Houses in Cressbrook start to pass into private ownership

1985 Listing of original Victorian buildings in Cressbrook

1997 Cressbrook school closes

2000 Cressbrook Mill renovated by David Holmes

Dark satanic mills?

The early 1800s were chaotic years in the industrial revolution. No laws covered the rights of the workers in factories leading to ruthless exploitation of vulnerable apprentices being reported

When Richard Arkwright senior died in 1792 a major portion of his estate, including all of his spinning interests were passed down to his son Richard Arkwright junior. Richard however, believing that better business prospects lay in other directions, decided to pull out of the spinning business altogether and sold his interests at Cressbrook to his uncle, Samuel Simpson. Simpson leased the mill to John Baker's son Edmund and his business partner Barker Bossley until Edmund Baker's early retirement due to ill-health in 1799. These were war years and a lean time for small business people like Barker Bossley, who were taxed heavily to support the war against Napoleon and whose

John Leigh Philips

access to raw materials and markets was restricted by the conflict. For a few years he struggled on his own to make the mill pay until he went bankrupt late in 1808 and production at the mill ceased.

Samuel Simpson put the mill and the entire Frith enclosure on the market and shortly after in 1810 the package was leased for £82 per year by JL Philips and Brother, Cotton Spinners, from Manchester. The Philipses used the mill for their own patented thread manufacturing processes while pursuing sport, hunting and fishing in the Frith. Not having the history of dispute with the Devonshire's that had limited what Arkwright could accomplish at the Frith, they obtained permission to create the mill pool at Water-cum-Jolly

as it now appears and used the significant increase in water force to drive a much bigger industrial complex. They re-employed William Newton as manager and with their money he commissioned the construction of Wye Mill, or *Big Mill* as it is known locally. Construction of the new mill commenced in 1814 and was completed at a cost of £12,000 which was considered a worthy investment following the end of the war in France and the consequent expansion of all industries, not just cotton. It is also likely that at this time the lower gradient road with the hairpin-bend in Ravensdale, which links Monsal Dale Road to the Litton Road, was built. This was to accommodate the commercial traffic for the mill which now traded to the north west via Whaley Bridge rather than, as before with Arkwright's other commercial interests toward the south. This is shown clearly in the construction of the White Gate, which is in the eastern wall of the mill complex. The gate is staggered back slightly on its northern side to

accommodate more easily traffic that was clearly predominantly leaving and entering the mill from the north, up into Ravensdale.

The new mill was powered by water flowing through a goyt from the new mill pool on the Wye. With the new mill having also been built across the original goyt from the Cress Brook, the waters from the new goyt were also fed into the existing wheel on Richard Arkwright's mill. The new complex could now accommodate many more workers to satisfy the greater manning requirements. Newton exploited the then weak employment laws to bring in as apprentices large numbers of pauper children from the slums of Bethnal Green in the East End of London and Westminster. To accommodate the children Newton

An artists impression of Arkwright's mill

About 1820

The gorge of Water-cum-jolly is now flooded with the mill-pool created by the new dam.

Rock House may have disappeared by this time and Newton moved into a house built into the end of Dale Terrace.

Both mills are fed from the same goyt.

who may have deemed the enterprise ill-conceived.

The early years of the industrial revolution were quite chaotic, with little in the way of legal control. In particular there were no laws covering the rights of workers in factories, or *manufactureys* as they were called at the time, as this way of working was entirely new. The way was thus open for unscrupulous entrepreneurs to exploit the lack of legislation ruthlessly and it has been well documented how the early success of the cotton mills was paid for with the lives of the pauper and orphan children who were coerced to work in them, often under atrocious conditions. The apprentice system, whereby young people were taken under indentures to train in a trade while assisting their employer, was a well-established and respected process and had been operating

successfully for centuries. Many of the new mill owners saw it only as a source of cheap labour however. The tight-packed nature of the spinning machinery meant that child labourers were very useful and could squeeze into the spaces between the machines to clear faults, blockages and the cotton fluff that was such a fire hazard.

Photograph courtesy of Picture The Past

The Wick - William Newton's cottages in Ravensdale

also built large a house that sits immediately to the north of the mill on the small lane which over the years has been known as Apprentice Row and Pancake Row, and is now known as both Dale Terrace and Dale View Terrace. It is also likely that at this time Newton moved from Rock House in Water-cum-Jolly to the building that is now called The Old School House at the eastern end of Dale Terrace as Rock House was inundated when the new mill pool was created. The lack of debris in the vicinity of Rubicon Wall suggests that the house was dismantled rather than abandoned. When a third mill was commissioned by the Philipses in 1823, Apprentice Row was expanded still further and acquired the gothic Western gable end that it now sports. The expansion of the accommodation in Apprentice Row

did not keep up with the staffing needs of the mills and for a while some of the apprentices were housed in the roof space of Wye Mill. The roof spaces in all of the mills were lit by large skylights, which enabled their gainful use.

With the staffing needs of the mills now running at around 400 apprentices and associated overseers, Newton asked the Philipses for money to build further accommodation around the corner from the mill in Ravensdale. They refused his requests so Newton funded this construction from his own pocket and let the houses to the salaried employees of the mill. These cottages have at some point acquired the name *Newton's Folly*. The precise reason for this name is not clear although it could have been coined by the Philipses,

About 1825

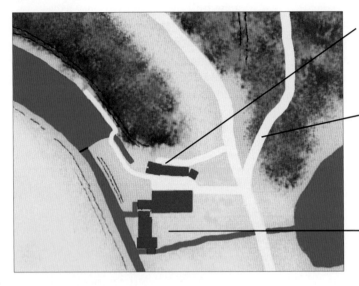

The Apprentice house is extended by the addition of the gothic west end.

A road is built into Ravensdale for mill traffic, going mainly to Manchester. This also provides access to the cottages in Ravensdale.

A third mill is added at the southern end of the original mill.

The spinning machinery was not protected by the gates and cages in place in modern factories, however, and many children lost their lives brutally in the flailing components. There is sufficient evidence to show that the apprentices who served at Cressbrook Mill were treated better than some. Strong and relevant comparisons, for example, can be made between the treatment of the apprentices at Cressbrook Mill and those at its neighbour, Litton Mill, as both were operating at the same time and were staffed in the same manner. Some controversy exists over the treatment meted out to the apprentices at Cressbrook as there are conflicting accounts of the conditions endured by the children who worked there. The following account of life at Cressbrook Mill by is recounted by

John Birley, who worked at both Litton and Cressbrook Mills. It is taken from an article written by James Rayner Stevens and was published in the Ashton Chronicle in 1849;

'The boys were told before they came here what sport they would have among the hills, catching the hares and the rabbits, and fishing in the brooks and streams. But we found ourselves sadly mistaken; for I have sometimes gone into the Frith, or the twitches on a summer's night, when the master has seen us or some one has told him, he used to send for us into the counting-house or cellar-room, half-a-dozen at a time, or as many as had been in the woods birdnesting. He would ask us what we had been doing there. We told him birdnesting or nutting. He would then

order the watchman, Hancock or Brown to go into Wardlow Wood for half-a-dozen hazel sticks. Then he ordered the watchman to strip us, made us mount on one another's backs, and would himself flog us with these hazel sticks across out bare buttocks and loins till he cut the flesh and made the blood flow. He also made us flog one another, and would stand over us to see that we laid on; and if we did not lay on hard enough, he laid on us himself.'

This brutal account is somewhat contradicted by an account by Dr Hawkins who inspected Cressbrook Mill on behalf of the Factories Commission. Dr Hawkins wrote;

'I must state to the honour of Mr Newton, that after a very minute and unexpected examination of his establishment, and of the apprentices in private, I could ascertain no point in their treatment that savoured of niggardliness nor of harshness. The remoteness of the situation, the distance from public opinion, the absence of parents and relations, all afford an opportunity for abuse, but that opportunity is not seized.'

Contradictions like this in contemporary accounts of the life of mill workers are quite common. They occur because the conditions in the mills and factories of England had by this time become a highly charged topic and the cause of the most

vulnerable and abused of the mill workers had been taken up by a number of noteworthy members of society who sought to introduce laws to protect them. These reformists used the more extreme accounts of abuse as propaganda to support their aims. Benevolent accounts of mill life, however, were exploited by anti-reformist mill owners who stood to lose most from the introduction of laws protecting the workforce. The evidence that these conflicting accounts represents must therefore be viewed very carefully. The truth almost inevitably lies somewhere between these two extremes but without doubt the working practices of the time were hard, even after reform. The apprentices who worked in the mills were highly vulnerable and most of them were working a long way away from any relatives that might have afforded them protection. Mills like Cressbrook were staffed by workhouse children who arrived on the back of promises of schooling, new opportunities and gainful employment. Their local boroughs were usually only too grateful to have their charges taken off their hands and both boys and girls were usually signed-on at the mills for a set period, although the high instance of illiteracy within their communities means that many of those taken on were unlikely to have understood fully the implications of the agreements they set their names or marks to. The children were subsequently transported to their

The dual water wheels of Wye Mill and Arkwright Mill

which would protect the workers. Michael Sadler of Snelston, Derbyshire, MP for Newark, was a stalwart defender of mill workers. Together with Lord Ashley and other reformists he campaigned for reform and eventually forced the government to draw up the Factory Act of 1833, which attempted to establish a normal working day for workers specifically in the textile industry. But the limits set were far from lenient and adult textile mill workers could still expect to start their working day at 5.30 am and work until 8.30 pm should the mill owner so wish. Employees aged 13 to 18 were afforded slightly more protection and could not be expected to work more than a 12 hour stretch, less an hour and a half for meals. Children aged nine to thirteen had a nine hour limit and nobody could be employed during the night.

Once again the new laws, while more stringent, were only introduced sporadically and at the discretion of the mill owners. To be fair, many complied - but many more did not. There were prosecutions and convictions, however, and gradually many owners did come round, although it took a number of further reforms of the Factories Act. Newton's efforts to staff the mills at Cressbrook were hampered by the passing of the Factories Acts but he exploited a loophole in the law to bring to Cressbrook the orphans of armed forces personnel killed in military campaigns from the Royal

place of work and in the absence of any guardian were often cruelly and disgracefully abused. Far too many did not live to see out their full term and return to their families. Many who did returned maimed, broken and witless. The changes in the law, which were to lead eventually to the workforce practices in place today, had their foundations in this early part of the 19th Century. A basic attempt was made at affording the vulnerable some protection with the 1802 Factories Act. This was a fairly primitive set of laws that did little more than specify the food, clothing and environmental requirements for factory workers

but in remote corners of the country there was an absence of governance and even these basic requirements were not enforced. A further reform in 1819 was similarly unsuccessful and ironically it was the new mass-production exploited by the mill owners that was to lead ultimately to the abolition of their cruel practices. This period saw the launch of a number of mass produced newspapers, many of which are still in production, including *The Times* (1814), *The Manchester Guardian* (1821) and *The Evening Standard* (1827). As has always been the case with the press, any opportunity to publish

controversial items to boost circulation was seized upon and the suffering of working children and women was a popular topic. Through the newspapers knowledge of the abuse became widespread and there emerged a will in many quarters to exert control on the mill owners to protect their employees from exploitation. The power to act against the problem, however, rested with the privileged few as the general populace at this time still had no vote, as electoral reform only started in 1832. It took the interest and intervention of concerned members of both houses of parliament to introduce the changes

above: Litton Mill

left: Matthew Dickies doubling sheds photographed in 1959

Photograph courtesy of English Heritage

Military Asylum in Chelsea. These children were not subject to the same protection that civilian children from the inner city workhouses were now afforded: this legal anomaly that successfully challenged in 1840. Although in charge of what appears to have been a benevolent regime, Newton's recruitment activities were also hampered by Cressbrook Mill's geographical proximity to Litton Mill, where Ellis Needham's brutal working practices stirred considerable anti-mill feelings in the local population. In raising objections to the recruitment of orphans to Litton, unfortunately they tarred Cressbrook with the same brush and in the 20 years that Newton was in charge at Cressbrook he fought running legal battles with the local magistratum and Lord Scarsdale over his rights to recruit apprentices. That Newton broke the law with his recruitment policies has never been proven, however.

During his time as mill manager for the Philipses, William Newton brought into the business his three sons, James, Edward and William junior. Edward appears to have played the role of book-keeper, James was tasked with the recruitment of a suitable workforce, while William junior was instantly interested in the mechanics and engineering of spinning. It was William jnr who played the key role in the establishment of Cressbrook as a successful cotton spinning interest, rather than his father. He oversaw

nearly all of the engineering concerns at the site, including the construction of the dam and mill-pool in Water-cum-Jolly and the construction of Wye Mill. He communicated regularly with his employers to secure the funding required to equip the mill and even managed to overcome the difficulties experienced by many mill owners in securing suitably high standard equipment by purchasing the machinery from a failed mill in Sheffield. William also designed and implemented new machinery to improve both the output and the quality of thread at Cressbrook. Neither William nor his father could be classed as engineers of particular note and could be considered at best as talented journeymen. Had they been highly skilled then the economics of the time would have allowed them to travel to almost any milling region in the country and name their price, such was the shortages of skilled craftsmen. It is probable that in Cressbrook they saw an opportunity to be gainfully and reliably employed, which is why their residence at the mill lasted the 25 years from the Philipses acquisition of the site in 1810 until its sale by them in 1835.

Following the sale of the mill to McConnel and company in 1835 the Newtons were released from Philipses employ.

William Newton snr died in 1830 and is buried along with his wife, Helen, in Tideswell.

WHO WERE JL PHILIPS AND BROTHER, COTTON SPINNERS?

John Leigh Philips and Francis Leigh Philips were brothers and cotton spinners from Mayfield in Manchester. The Philips family were established and leading industrialists when they came to Cressbrook in 1810 and had been trading since the middle of the 17th Century. John and Francis inherited their grandfather Nathaniel Philips' silk spinning business and operated it independently of the family's main interest, Philips and Lee, Cotton Spinners, which had been set up by Sir George Philips and George Lee some years previously.

John was a volunteer commanding officer who eventually rose to the rank of Lieutenant Colonel and led both the 1st and 2nd Battalions, Manchester and Salford Volunteer Infantry until the disbanding of voluntary corps in 1802. He was also a founding member in 1785 of the Manchester

Contemporary illustration of the 'Peterloo' Massacres

Literary and Philosophical Society and published a number of works on poetry and natural history through them. Before his death on the 23rd June 1814, John Leigh Philips petitioned widely to a number of notable military personnel and noble patrons to gain promotion for his son John, then a midshipman. Between 1810 and 1814, John Jnr saw active service against the French on the vessels HMS Jamaica, Bombay and Trusty. His father's persistence paid off in 1815 when he was promoted to Lieutenant on board HMS Falcon, but his career was to be limited following the defeat of Napoleon's forces in 1814 and the general stand-down of military personnel. Following John snr's death, son John returned home and joined his uncle Francis in running the family business, which included interests in thread spinning, tape spinning and plantations in North America.

In 1819, just after the event, Francis Philips wrote a book entitled *An exposure of the calumnies* circulated by the enemies of social order and reiterated by their abettors against the Yeoman cavalry of Manchester and Salford in which he defended the actions of the militia in the so-called Peterloo Massacres at St Peter's Field in Manchester. This was the militia that his brother had served in with distinction for so many years. John Philips jnr died in 1835. His uncle and business partner Francis lost interest in spinning at Cressbrook and returned to Bank Hall in Mayfield, Manchester. He put the mill and the Frith on the open market, much to the distress of William Newton jnr.

St James Piccadilly Board of Governors   May 1816

It having been resolved at the last Board to Apprentice Boys and Girls from the Workhouse and Parish School of Industry to Manufacturers and Messrs Phillips and Co of Cressbrook in the parish of Tideswell in the County of Derby having applied to the Board for several Boys and Girls as Apprentices, And this Board having received very satisfactory information by letters from the Rev Thomas Brown Minister of the Parish of Tideswell and from A.A.Shuttleworth one of the Magistrates, Justices of the Peace of the County of Derby, resident near to said Manufactory speaking highly of the treatment and management of the Children apprenticed to said Manufactory and having other sufficient and satisfactory information to the same effect particularly as to the attention paid to the Morals of said Apprentices Did authorize and order that the undermentioned Boys and Girls be Apprenticed to said Manufactory or any other of equal suitability and kind treatment

Boys	Girls
Richard Blay	Elizabeth Mansell
Richard Dalby	Elizabeth Teague
James Maliar	Mary Ann Carr
Chas Day	Julia Dyne
John Fisher	Isabella Williams
John McCoy	Hannah Debenham
John Marrian	Sophia Curtis
Thomas Blankley	Sarah Moore
John Timken	Caroline Fellows

A copy of a transcript from records of the Board Of Governors of the St James School of Industry releasing children to James Newton as apprentices at Cressbrook Mill in 1816

Source: City of Westminster Archives, Local Studies Library

THE EARLY CRESSBROOKIANS - CENSUS REPORTS FROM 1841

The first accurate record we have of early Cressbrookians is the 1841 census. The records show some 300 people at this stage were living in 51 homes which had been built in the last few years by Henry McConnel to house his workers. This was by now an economic solution as the cost of keeping apprentices had risen from 3/6d a week in 1815 to 14/6d a week. The cost of building a house at about £40 was a negligible proportion of the cost of equipping a mill. A typical house could be home to eleven, eight of whom were working family members and two lodgers, also employed at the mill. There were many such lodgers in Cressbrook identified as being born outside Derbyshire and thus is the last of the large army of pauper children brought in to man the mills.

Arkwright in the original mill had recruited locally from Nottingham and Manchester but the exponential growth of the cotton industry meant that all subsequent owners from Barker Bossley onwards had to look elsewhere. The parishes of London were willing suppliers and in fact advertised to that effect. Newton drew apprentices from St Giles, St. Andrews Marylebone, Clerkenwell and later St James Piccadilly.

In May 1816 St James Piccadilly sent their first batch of 18 children to Cressbrook and by October 1816 Cressbrook employed 158 children out a total of 250, the balance being labourers who were for the most part ex-apprentices. The apprentices earned 6d to a shilling per week 'encouragement' money. The labourers were paid 20-25 shillings a week. The working week was 6am to 8pm 6 days a week and they were supposed to go to church in Tideswell on Sunday.

By October 1819 St James had sent 50 apprentices to Cressbrook of whom two, John Morrison and Caroline Fellows had previously worked at a mill near Macclesfield which had burnt down. Three of the original consignment had died and Newton was now asking for 10 or 12 females *with an allowance for cloathes*.

Since 1816 parishes had been forbidden sending children more than 40 miles away. The reason for this was that the majority of these children were not orphans as usually described and so could be permanently separated from their worried parents so the mill had to look elsewhere for labour. The Duke of York's school of the Royal Military Asylum Chelsea who looked after and educated the children of soldiers and sailors was not covered by the legislation and so could send 49 children to Cressbrook between 1826 and 1836, initially to Newton and later to the McConnels.

Cressbrook was one of the last cotton mills in Derbyshire if not the UK to continue to use child labour. The Derbyshire *Return of Apprentices in Cotton Mills December 1840* shows that of 137 apprentices in Derbyshire 66 were in Cressbrook. The next largest group was 31 in equally isolated Edale.

Since 1841 over half the original families had left to be replaced by other workers. Typical of these were the Broomheads from Litton, a family of 14 of whom nine worked at the mill, the youngest only 11 years old. The younger children did however now get some education as a teacher, James Wills, had arrived from Sheffield. After 1844 children under the age of 13 were restricted to 'half time' work, that is $6^{1/2}$ hours a day with three hours at school. Or they could have five hours of school on three alternate days.

JOHN BIRLEY

OUT OF SUFFERING COMES REFORM

The nineteenth century was one of considerable political upheaval. During this time marked differences in political doctrine became apparent with strong camps both in support of maintaining the status quo and in favour of wide-reaching reforms. The suffering of manual labourers in all primary industries was a cornerstone of the arguments for and against reform and the published accounts of life in Cressbrook and Litton mills by John Birley and his contemporaries like Robert Blincoe, were instrumental in raising the political temperature through publication in the rapidly expanding press. This disaffection was exploited by the reformists to mobilise the then disenfranchised population against the often exploitative regime under which they toiled and by whom they were heavily taxed. In particular, Manchester had become a strong industrial centre and a focus for much of the unrest. This manifested itself at St Peter's Fields in Manchester in 1819 when a political husting addressed by key reformers of the day was violently dispersed by members of the local yeomanry resulting in 12 dead and over 400 wounded. Many acts of political reformation were passed in the latter half of the century, including those that protected the workforce and those that were to eventually bring the vote to the general population.

> " *At the mill [Litton Mill] the Dale becomes impassable, at least for carriages, and we had therefore to take up a remarkably steep hill to get to Cressbrook. About three parts up this lofty eminence we had a most magnificent view of an immense district to the south-east and west ... The great Finn and Longstone Edge appeared right and left of us. In the distance the lofty hills around Chatsworth, Haddon, Winster, Matlock, with the multitude of lovely vales that isolate them, and adorn and distinguish Derbyshire, are laid beneath the eye of the spectator like a splendid picture. The Dale connecting Miller's and Cressbrook [Water-cum-Jolly] seems to be beneath your feet. The best point to view this seems to be about two hundred yards below the plantation. We moved on through this and soon got into a good road leading from Tideswell to Cressbrook.*
>
> *The proprietor of Cressbrook Mill has built here some beautiful cottages in the Swiss style, for his work-people, on the very brow of the lofty hill overlooking Cressbrook, which have a charming effect amid this truly alpine scenery; and, thanks to this spirited gentleman, the roads are excellent, and although taken down the fearful steep bounding Cressbrook, where the whole is covered with luxuriant plantations, with the drag on, we bowled down in fine style and soon passed the extensive mill of Cressbrook, and the house of the proprietor (McConnell, Esq). It is a wonderful structure in such a position, for we seem here shut in on all sides, apparently far, very far from the great world. It is indeed a romantic spot ....* "

William Adam's account of his visit by coach to Cressbrook, published in the fifth edition of his book *Gem of the Peak* in 1851.

Self-interested charity

The 1840s saw the start of a purpose-built village for his workers by an unusually caring employer, Henry McConnel

Rock House, the beginning of the model village

In 1835 the Philips interests in Cressbrook were purchased by McConnel and Company for lace thread production to supply the booming lace trade in Nottingham. Conversion of the mill for McConnel's proprietary lace thread took two years and local production started in 1837. James and Henry McConnel came to Cressbrook from Ancoats in

Around 1838/6

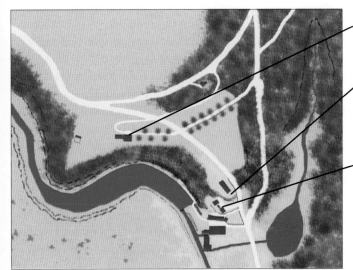

Henry McConnel has built Cressbrook Hall.

Rock House, the first of the houses that are to become McConnels model village.

The developments at the mill now also includes the buildings of Cressbrook Farm (now known as Home Farm)

Manchester with an established reputation for caring for their workforce through the provision at their own expense of housing, Sunday schools, medical treatment and sick pay. They were reported upon favourably by the same government select committees that had pilloried the likes of Litton Mill in the lead up to the Factories Acts. The McConnels'

roots were working class and they were very much part of the nouveau riche that the industrial revolution created. They had inherited the company business from their father, James McConnel. James jnr bought a patch of land in the Polygon area of Ardwick, near Manchester and built himself a family home. Henry was taken with Cressbrook and the area around the Frith; so much so that he immediately set about making the place his home and commissioned the design and construction of Cressbrook House, as it was then called. The house was accessed by two coach roads with gradients more sympathetic to horse drawn vehicles. These permitted easier access up the hill to the house and beyond to Newton's road to Litton.

The records of the Royal Military Asylum show that the McConnels, in the person of Henry's wife Isabella McConnel, still had contact with the sources engaged by James Newton to staff the mills. Although Henry McConnel brought with him a

professional labour force from their existing mills in Manchester and employed people from both Litton and Tideswell, he also inherited the Philips' apprentice workforce. Rather than dispensing with their services, however, he allowed those that wished to see out their apprenticeships to stay. Even within Cressbrook today there is living memory of the last of the apprentices, a lady who remained in the village after her apprenticeship finished and lived here until her death at the age of 92.

McConnel housed his workforce initially in the houses in Dale Terrace, in Newton's cottages in Ravensdale, or *The Wick* as it is still known and in houses in the local villages. As beautiful and entrancing as the

CRESSBROOK HALL

In 1835 Henry McConnel commissioned the design of a great hall to stand on the bluff overlooking Water-cum-Jolly and the mill and created around it parkland in the manner of the great houses of the time. McConnel spared no expense on the house and turned to the great notaries of the times for its design and construction. Cressbrook House, as it was called then, was designed by the notable architect Thomas Johnson from Lichfield while the gardens were laid out by Edward Kemp, a student of Joseph Paxton at Chatsworth House, who was a major and lasting influence on garden design. The house is built to an irregular L-plan on three floors using vermiculated gritstone blocks and gritstone dressings with limestone extensions to the west, all under Welsh slate roofs with moulded gritstone chimneys, grouped in stacks of 2,3,4 and 5. The north elevation has a central gabled bay which encloses an oak doorway above which is the McConnell coat of arms with the motto 'Victor in Arduis' (Triumph in adversity). The south elevation has a

centre bay with three, four-centred arches to the ground floor with four light mullioned windows above and to the west is a two-story building bearing a date-stone of 1851. This was originally the billiard room and was connected to the main building by an Orangery which was restored in 2001. McConnel was also an early patron of Turner and purchased a number of his works for display in his new house with its ornate plaster ceilings, Italian marble fireplaces and curved oak staircase. Two special roads were built to the house that followed easier gradients than the road straight up the hill. These allowed for access by horse-drawn carriage and past the house rejoined Newton's road to Litton.

transferred back to McConnel's other mills in Manchester. Faced with this unhappiness and probably seeing the advantages of accommodating his workforce within easy walking distance of the mill, McConnel commissioned the construction of three tiers of beautiful, stone built houses for his workforce. The three tiers were called Lower Wood, Middle Row and Upper Wood, although Upper Wood Cottages have for some time now been known as Top Cottages. Often described in contemporary publications as 'in a Swiss style', the houses were built on the south facing flanks of the hill, above both the Frith and Henry McConnel's house, catching the sun. The view from all of the houses is over the mill and along the length of Upper Dale, toward Headstones; spectacular indeed. The access roads that had been built to permit easier access to the hall were extended up the hill to reach the houses in the new development and also linked up with the Litton road. Seizing upon a business opportunity, McConnel also opened the road through the estate to tolled traffic and built a toll house at the bottom end of Middle Row for the collection of fees. This house is still

The Toll House

referred to as the Toll House.
The precise dates for the commencement of the work on the new houses is undocumented but the census records of 1841 show that they were occupied by this time, suggesting that they were built quite soon after McConnel arrived. In all other things, Henry McConnel revealed himself as a thoroughly modern and up-to-date gentleman and this is demonstrated in the design patterns of his house, his village and the Lodge Houses built later on the estate. The designs of each are utterly typical of the day and follow closely the recommendations carried in contemporary publications like the *Encyclopaedia of Cottage, Farm and Villa Architecture and Furniture* by J C Loudon, which includes a design for *A Cottage Dwelling In The German Swiss Style*. So it was that at a time when the manufacture of larger panes of glass, and thus larger windows, was becoming both inexpensive and commonplace, the houses instead used stone mullioned windows with small diamond panes. A highly romanticised design that could be mistaken at a glance for one perhaps 200 years older

cottages in the Wick are, their location in a deep declivity sandwiched between on one side the dense woodland of the Frith and on the other the imposing ramparts of Ravens Crag, gives the cottages a claustrophobic feel. The light down in the Wick is feel. The light down in the Wick is

often only strong when the sun is full in the south and both mornings and evenings find the cottages in the shade. McConnel's workforce was unhappy with its life down in the Wick, so much so that they nicknamed it *Bury-me-wick* and many asked to be

and absolutely typical of the ordered approach to romantic building favoured by the wealthy during this period. If the designs were retro, then the finishing was modern and the window closures were of contemporary caste iron and were fitted with polished brass furniture. The main construction of the houses was of random limestone with stepped gritstone coins protecting the corners of the buildings while the chimneys were slender, elegant columns of gritstone and the blue slate roofs sported large, ornate finials at the gable points. The Stone Pit at the top of the village from which the main building materials for the houses was dug is still in use today.

The houses were made in a variety of sizes with those he inherited in the Wick being the smallest. The accommodation in Upper Wood and Middle Row were of a similar size while the biggest houses were in Lower Wood, although at some point since their construction the Lower Wood houses have been reorganised internally. Flying freeholds and party walls in which can be found old bricked-up doorways are both evidence of a reorganisation of the accommodation into smaller and more versatile packages.

As landlords and estate managers the McConnels allocated the accommodation to their workforce and moved them around according to their housing needs. Newly weds were first accommodated in the small cottages in the Wick and were only moved up into the newer and larger houses as they had children and the size of the families grew.

Henry McConnel retired in 1860 and James jnr followed him shortly after in

Around 1850

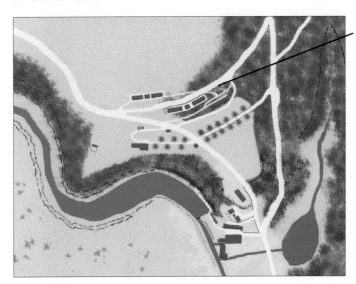

The main part of the village has been built, together with the accommodation lodges at the hall.

1861, leaving their brother William in sole directorship. Henry McConnel enjoyed a warm relationship with his workforce and tenants and never forgot his working class roots. On his retirement he was presented with a glowing eulogy by the workers of the mill in which they expressed their thanks and appreciation for the care with which he conducted his patronage. The eulogy is still in the possession of Cressbrook Institute and hangs there. An indication of the sensitivity of the man and perhaps a hint of the nature that made him

such a philanthropist can be found in the words that he himself chose to describe his father, James McConnel snr, who founded the company that Henry and his brother inherited;

'My father was, in business matters, pains-taking and persevering rather than acute. He possessed common sense rather than talent, was thoughtful, prudent and even somewhat timid, rather than impulsive or rash. In society he shrank from putting himself forward, and was perhaps a little too sensitive as to the good opinion of others; but when amongst friends the expression of his natural kindness of disposition was unrestrained, and he was warm hearted and genial in manner and fond of innocent mirth.'

Upper Wood Cottages

The McConnel Eulogy was almost consigned to the bonfire after being discovered 15 years ago by Ron and Una Hill - it was being used to cover a hole in the roof to keep the rain out of Cressbrook Club. The newly restored and reframed part of Cressbrooks history was unveiled by Una Hill at Cressbrook Club in June 2005 with many Cressbrook residents - old and new - coming to view a piece of village history not seen for many years.

Values and attributes that could perhaps have been credited to Henry McConnel himself.

Henry McConnel died in 1871 when the mill was still in the administration of his brother William. The village continued to be administered by his estate and his daughter, Mary Worthington and later by her son Henry Hugo Worthington. Mary Worthington in particular took a keen interest in carrying on her father's role as patron to the village.

The now large industrial complex of the mill and the associated village created a significant and expanding local population, the children of which presented the Worthingtons with a problem with respect to schooling. Although Litton, Tideswell and Great Longstone had schools that could accommodate the older children, they were not convenient for the people in Cressbrook or the youngest of their children. Mary Worthington's solution was to fund the construction of a purpose-built school, which was situated at the very end of Dale Terrace. The school opened in 1878 and James McConnel was at times a trustee, with his signature appearing regularly in the school logs now located with the Derbyshire Records Office in Matlock.

1878 also saw the start of a period of significant change for the mill when William McConnel retired and his son John W McConnel was appointed director of the company. In Nottingham, the lace industry had long

passed its peak and with demand dropping off, Cressbrook Mill was incorporated as a separate commercial entity from McConnel and Company and started trading as Cressbrook Mills Company Ltd. The 1881 census reveals that very few people living in the village were left working at the mill after the partition so there must have been a great number of redundancies. The census also shows that fortunately most people who remained in the village had also managed to find other occupations and incomes.

The mill was let to Lord Scarsdale,

who also operated the mill at Litton at this time. Lord Scarsdale appointed Greg Brothers of Styal, another very large and successful spinning concern, as Managing Directors of the mill and Charles Edward Solly was the mill manager. Solly died tragically young and in his memory Mary Worthington funded the building of a stone seat on the hill halfway up to the village to allow people to rest on their way back from work. The inscription on the seat reads as follows;

In memory of
CHARLES EDWARD SOLLY
For 8 years in charge of
The Cressbrook Mill
Died 5th January 1898 aged 33
The Memory of the Just is Blessed

The seat was restored in 1998. Charles Solly lived in Rock House on the end of Rock Cottages overlooking the river with a housemaid and cook called Harriet Sutton. Rock House is a particularly attractive house with a mullioned bay window in the south gable. The view, from it's flat garden, is quite breathtaking as it looks out over the top of the mill to the south and to Putty Hill to the west. The interior of the house still has original prestigious features distinguishing it as a more important house in the village. It still has the original mullioned windows with attractive diamond glass detail, large skirting boards and architraves and proper brass door handles rather than latches into the main rooms.

above: An early view of the road into Monsal Dale

Solly's seat

A buggy parked outside Home Farm with Rock House further up the hill

25

WHO WERE THE MCCONNELS?

James McConnel was born in Kirkudbright in 1762. In 1781, together with his friend and neighbour John Kennedy, he was apprenticed to his uncle, William Cannan who had established a machine-making business at Chowbent, near Leigh in Lancashire. After serving a period in apprenticeship and a further period in the employ of a weft and twist trader called Egelsom in Manchester, McConnel and Kennedy went into partnership in 1791 with brothers Benjamin and William Sandford. The Sandford brothers provided capital investment while McConnel and Kennedy provided engineering expertise for a cotton spinning and machine manufacturing partnership. This lasted four years before

McConnel and Kennedy set up on their own as McConnel and Kennedy & Co at Shooter's Brook in 1795.

The early years were split between lucrative business of machine manufacture and of cotton spinning but by the turn of the 19th century, the firm had switched its business base firmly to spinning, which by then was more profitable than engineering though the firm continued to manufacture spare parts for both their own machinery and that of their customers.

Much of the early success was generated by sales in the Scottish yarn market but a significant quantity also went to trade in European markets such as Russia, the Baltic states, Serbia and Switzerland as well as India and the far East. Trade with Prussia was accomplished by smuggling through British occupied Heligoland, which avoided both Napoleon's attention and prohibitive import duties. The company thus survived the lean years of the Napoleonic conflict largely on the merit of the high quality of its products and was well placed to exploit the surge in market growth that followed the peace.

James McConnel Senior

JAMES McCONNEL
Born August 11th 1803   Died March 2nd 1879

John Kennedy retired from the business in 1826 but retained a keen interest in engineering and joined the Manchester Literary and Philosophical Society. His only son opted not to follow his father into the business so John was replaced by James McConnel's sons Henry and James jnr. The firm also changed its name at this point to McConnel & Co. James McConnel snr passed away on the 3rd of September 1831, shortly before the firm came to Cressbrook, at which point the third brother, William, also joined the business.

McConnel & Co capitalised on its

European successes by expanding into the English and Irish markets. The firm exploited the growth in demand for lace thread caused by the growth of the Nottingham lace trade by purchasing in 1835 the mill at Cressbrook, which they converted for the exclusive production of high quality doubled thread for this market. At this time McConnel and Company was the single biggest private company in the country, employing nearly 1,600 people.

Despite very difficult trading circumstances between 1837 and 1843, where factory-based manufacturing

Another view of Rock House from William Newtons access roads

HENRY McCONNEL
Born July 16th 1801   Died September 28th 1871

WILLIAM McCONNEL
Born August 31st 1809   Died October 10th 1902

J. W. McCONNEL
Born 14th February 1855

was disrupted by the Chartist riots, the firm maintained its market position and in 1851, along with four other cotton spinning firms, purchased the patent for a revolutionary combing machine made by Heilmann, which only strengthened further McConnel's position in the quality thread market. John Kennedy died in 1855 and in 1860 Henry McConnel retired to Cressbrook Hall. James retired a year later leaving William in sole charge. There were lean years for the whole of the cotton industry during the American Civil War, which began in 1861 and which significantly affected

the import of the high quality raw Sea Island Cotton that the business preferred in its manufacture of the highest quality cotton threads. The imports did not recover until 1865 but William McConnel had had the foresight to stock up with considerable raw stock prior to the war and managed to operate the mills more or less fully during this time, unlike some of his competitors.

The next fifteen years were very successful under William's guidance and he retired in 1878, passing control to his son John W McConnel. John partitioned the McConnel's business

interests at Cressbrook in 1893 and let them first to Lord Scarsdale and then to Matthew Dickie jnr Ltd, although Henry's daughter Mary continued to live at Cressbrook Hall for a number of years.

In 1897 McConnel & Co joined with a number of likeminded businesses to form the Fine Spinners Association but retained its McConnel identity until John retired after the First World War. It thereupon became incorporated within the general amalgamation of spinning interests, with the firm's assets eventually being acquired by Courtaulds with whom they remain.

Water-cum-Jolly Dale
A Swiss Photocrom of 1890 by the
Detroit Publishing company

right: An early engraving of
Cressbrook Mill and the village

THE EARLY CRESSBROOKIANS CENSUS REPORTS FROM 1851

By 1851 the Mill employed 83 men, 142 women, 58 boys and 46 girls and by now the boys and girls were the children of the adult employees. Of the original families who remained, many were to stay until 1901 and so perhaps were original Cressbrookian. The Bagshaws for example, are listed as local landowners on the enclosure map of 1764 and the Skidmores are recorded in the earliest census with Thomas being born in Cressbrook in 1806 and his wife Mary in 1811. Other long staying families were the Heathcotes and Harrisons in Ravensdale and the Jacksons, Sellars and Walkers.

The 1861 Census report shows Cressbrook village had 377 residents living in 75 households - which made an average of 5 people per house. Although large families were normal for the period only two families, the Wigleys and the Chadwicks had nine children each. Surprisingly, there were 12 one-child households and 1 three-children households. School age appeared to be from 3-16 and school was a large room at the top of the village overlooking Water-cum-Jolly Dale. There were 70 school children in the village and 80% were nine or younger. It was not until 1878 that Mary Worthington arranged for a purpose-built school close to the mi

There were a further 63 children in the village aged 9 -18 who were working, the majority at the mill, which employed 160 village residents. Other jobs in the village included: farm bailiff, 17 railway labourers, (construction had started in 1860 of the rail link from Rowsley to Buxton) table-blade forger, booker, agricultural labourer, grocer/draper, shop assistant, tailor, stone mason, artist and apprentice, charwoman, coachman, postman, gardeners, domestic servant, shoe maker, lead miners and a blacksmith, although there was no doctor, nurse or midwife.

Of the adult population aged 18 years and over, women outnumbered the men 55% to 45%. However, if the men lived beyond 55 years old they outnumbered the women. Extraordinarily, the oldest male resident in this 1861 census was a 73-year-old retired lead miner and the oldest female a retired 80-year-old houseservant. Older mums were represented by Milicent Bradley who at the age of 42 gave birth to her daughter Mary. The Wigley family had nine children aged 3-17, with no mother and the eldest daughter Ellen working as housekeeper. Four of the family aged 10 –15 worked at the mill, three aged four to seven were at school and a three year old boy was at home. The father, Joshua aged 40 was a widower and worked, in the gas house at the mill which was a less than

healthy place to work but the slightly higher pay would have been attractive to a man who had no sick pay, no pension and a young dependent family. John Arnold was the schoolmaster, a Sheffield-born man aged 35. He was married to Elisabeth who was also from Sheffield and a schoolmistress. They had obviously moved around as their older children were born in Cornwall, Northampton and Manchester. The younger children Edith three and George aged one were born in Cressbrook, indicating that they had been at the school for about 4 years by the time the census was taken. They had seven children altogether aged 1-13, with the 5-13 year-olds all at school. Elisabeth is listed as a schoolmistress and there is no live-in home help, so the youngest must have been looked after while she taught. The Arnolds were both still teaching at Cressbrook school in the 1871 census, showing that they lived and taught in the village for at least 14 years. Many of the orphan apprentices had been brought from Chelsea and Middlesex Parishes. The Doddemeades were both London apprentices, Henry from St

James' Piccadilly and Jane from St Luke's, Chelsea. Henry was a warehouseman in the Mill and his name appears on the village Eulogy for Henry McConnel in 1867. When Jane, the first wife of Henry Doddemeade, was a retired mill worker, they had seven children aged 12 –26 and twin grandchildren living at home. Of the six working children, five were at the mill and the youngest child was still at school. By the 1871 census, Henry then aged 64 had married Mary Walker aged 45, the widow of an overlooker at the mill and they had had a further two children.

The McConnel family lived at Cressbrook Hall, which on census day in 1861 was occupied by McConnel and his wife, two daughters, a visiting sister-in-law, a nephew who studied at Cambridge University, a governess from Birmingham, a butler, a groom, a cook, a ladies' maid, a housemaid, a kitchen maid and a laundress and at Lower Lodge a master gardener. The Hall butler William Wotten, was counted at the Hall, while his wife Elisabeth aged 56, lived down at Rock Cottages on her own. In the 1861 census Elisabeth was a very popular

name, in fact there were 20 'Elisabeths' in the village.

The 1881 census showed how the village's change from being just a dormitory for the mill was accelerating. The mill was now operated by Edward Gregg & Co employing only 80 people and yet there were still about 180 people of working age in the village, despite there being empty properties. Only seven wives were working, but surprisingly only one man described himself as a mill worker 'out of employment'. Occupations now included a butcher, labourer, cordwainer, cotton-weaver, farmer, butler, housekeeper, kitchen maid, housepainter - six in one house, gardener, cashier, lead miner employing 7 men, mill manager, frame-knitters, joiner, cotton winders, station master, farm bailiff, signalman, limers, limestone getters, fruit dealer, weaver of calico, errand boys, char woman, power-loom weaver, overlooker, grocer, general shop keeper and mill minders. Farming was popular as two neighbours both formerly 'overlookers of power-loom weavers' became farmers. William Lomas at 52 moved into Leisure Farm with 14 acres and Richard Walker was farming 43 acres. For the first time the Chapel House was identified as occupied by John David Jackson who was born in the village and at 24 was described as a 'cotton weaver and local Methodist preacher'.

Life in a model village

From the 1890s until the mill closed in 1965, the village was a fully functioning, working community with a shop, post office and visiting tradespeople

The 1890s were troubled times, often marked by general industrial shut-downs caused by a shortage of coal brought about by miners' strikes. Textile industries, which at this time were converting from water power to steam power, suffered along with everyone else. It was during a lay-off in 1893 from the mill in Stockport at which he worked that Matthew Dickie Jnr came on the off-chance to Wyedale and discovered the two mills at Litton and Cressbrook. At this time both mills were still powered by the river Wye and not vulnerable to the stoppages being played out in the steam-powered mills. Seeing an opportunity, he approached Lord Scarsdale and arranged to lease Litton Mill and sub-lease Cressbrook Mill for an initial period of 14 years. Together with his business partner William Mallison he formed Matthew Dickie Jnr Limited. The cost of the lease was underwritten by William Chaloner and William Johnson of Stockport, who became sleeping partners. The company started trading in 1894 and continued the tradition first started at Cressbrook by JL Philips & Brother in spinning and doubling high quality thread for the luxury end of the textile market.

above: Official company seal for Matthew Dickie Jnr Limited

right: Institute Row, now known as Hall View

One of Matthew Dickie's first actions was to agree with the McConnels to dispense with the water wheels that had to-date characterised and driven the development of the factory system during the industrial revolution. With their permission Dickie installed a modern, electricity generating water-turbine. This powered electric motors, which replaced the drive shafts and belts from the water wheels and made the power distribution around the mill more flexible. At the same time Mary Worthington arranged with Dickie for the installation of a private electricity distribution network in the village, making Cressbrook one of the first villages in the UK to benefit from a distributed electricity supply. The electricity cables were carried up the hill on poles while at the top of the village the cables were carried along and between the lines of houses on iron brackets attached to the upper stories. The kitchens and living rooms in the houses were fed with electricity and provided their occupants with electric light. The power was turned on between 4pm and 10pm during the week and between 4pm and 11pm on the weekends. Its cost was included with the rent and deducted from the wages of the tenant mill workers. Mary Worthington financed the building of the Institute Row, which commenced in 1899. Institute Row is so named because one of the houses in the row was given over explicitly as a community facility in the same manner as Working Men's Clubs in other industrial villages. The houses in the row are by some margin the biggest in

Around 1905

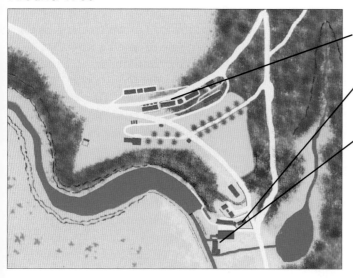

Institute Row and the Toll House are added

The school has been built

The mills no longer have water wheels, having been converted to water turbines

the village and were possibly built to replace the larger accommodation in Lower Wood, which had been previously divided up into smaller parcels. Institute Row is now mostly referred to as Hall View. When the houses in the upper village were first built they had neither running fresh water nor sewerage. Fresh water was fetched by pail from a nearby spring along what is now known as Cold Lane; a path that leads from the village and north into

The old water wheel and weir

the Frith in Ravensdale. Mary Worthington's solution to the fresh water problem was to build a water-powered pump below a weir on the Wye just upstream from Water-cum-Jolly and adjacent to a handy fresh-water spring. The weir funnelled water through a narrow goyt into the water wheel and as it turned it pumped fresh water from the spring, up the hill to holding tanks above the village. The water was fed to the houses via a network of cast-iron pipes, some of which can be still be seen and occasionally dug up. The pump was still in service during the early part of the 20th century before being replaced by a petrol driven pump and later still by the arrival of mains water to the village. The old water wheel, which has fallen into disrepair somewhat, can

still be seen on the weir in Water-cum-Jolly half way between Litton and Cressbrook Mills. The cottages in Ravensdale, meanwhile, continued to obtain their water from the springs in the Frith into the 1950s and the spring tap at the end of the row still flows to this day. Mary Worthington also installed the sewerage system still used by the cottages of Lower Wood, Middle Row and Upper Wood. During this time the village established itself as a fully-functioning community with shops, a Post Office and regular visits from passing

Lines on the opening of the new waterworks at Cressbrook by Mrs Worthington, the donor

Our village wears an aspect gay,
Let us rejoice - for well we may -
And greet the lady who today
Turns on the aqua pura.

A long-felt want is now supplied,
For hitherto we've been denied
The blessings reaching far and wide,
Which spring from aqua pura.

No more we'll murmur at our lot,
And say, "we surely are forgot",
Because enough we have not got
Of good, clean aqua pura.

No more our boys and girls shall slave.
No more we mothers scold and rave.

For plenty and to spare we'll have
Of healthful aqua pura.

We'll give our heartfelt thanks to those
Who did so kindly interpose
To lessen our domestic woes
By bringing aqua pura.

Within the reach of everyone,
Yea, verily, to our doorstone,
All are supplied, and now need none
Be short of aqua pura.

Then let the aqua pura flow,
Gaining in force as it doth go,
and we will reap the gain we know
Is had from aqua pura.

a poem written by Mrs Jane Bennett,
resident of Cressbrook April 1894

tradespeople. White's Directory of Derbyshire reports that William Froggatt was a 'grocer, draper, druggist, and ale and porter merchant' in Cressbrook. The area had also already become a popular rambling destination and walkers arrived regularly on the train at weekends to walk in the area. The farm at Upperdale offered teas and refreshments and a sweet shop operated on Dale Terrace.

Mary Worthington continued to act as benefactor to the village until she died in 1904 whereupon Henry Worthington took over the administration of the estate. The notable absence of significant additions to the structure of the village

since the building of Mary Worthington's Institute Row is an indication that he perhaps lacked the social ingenuity and invention that characterised his grandfather's and his mother's patronage.

Dickie and Mallison's venture meanwhile was successful. The firm extended its first lease in 1904 then again 1918 for another 19 years. They also acquired further mills in the Stockport area. Around this time, to overcome the seasonal impact that the variable water height in the river could have on production at the mill, the water turbine was replaced by a steam turbine, finally removing the mill from its dependence on the river that had so strongly influenced its original situation and subsequent development. The mill had an already established pattern of coal delivery using the railway and Henry McConnel had been instrumental in persuading the railway committee to build a station at Upperdale.

The gates going into the mill in 1959 showing the zig-zag roof of the main doubling rooms

Photograph courtesy of English Heritage

Something that was not present in the original design for the railway through Wyedale. The coal for many years was fetched by hand from where it was dumped from the train at the station using a horse and cart and shovels. Only later was it fetched by lorry. Following its conversion to steam turbine, the consumption of coal at the mill jumped immediately from the 400 or so tons per year that had been used to heat the buildings and create the coal gas for the thread-gassing process to over 1500 tons per year.

Henry Hugo Worthington died in March 1924 after which his son, Hugo Worthington and the remainder of the family decided not to continue in Cressbrook. William Mallison took the opportunity then to rent from the Worthington estate Cressbrook Hall, taking up residence in September 1924. When the Hall was put onto the open market in March the following year he bought it outright. Matthew Dickie in the meantime was in residence at Ravenstor House, to the west of Litton Mill. The company also bought out the remainder of the McConnel and Worthington interests in Cressbrook through a loan granted to them by the Worthingtons themselves. So it was that the village and its assets passed finally out of the McConnel legacy.

The depression of the 1930s hit Matthew Dickie Jnr Ltd extremely hard indeed and in 1933 the company approached Robert Henry Bingham, a wealthy farmer from Buxton, for a

loan. The cottages of Upper Wood and of Middle Row were set up as security against the loan as well as land on the northern side of Middle Row that included the War Memorial. Dickie also approached The Stanton Estate Company for money. This was duly granted with the remaining village assets and a 50% stake in the mill itself being put up against it as security.

Matthew Dickie died in 1936 with the extremely difficult trading conditions of the time continuing to cause the company serious financial trouble and the mill to run at a loss. An elective cut in pay by the workforce only temporarily staved off the inevitable and the company eventually went into liquidation. Despite the appointment of both a receiver and an external manager the mill could not continue and went bust on January 29th 1938. Robert Bingham and The Stanton Estate Company had no choice but to foreclose on the advances that had been made to Matthew Dickie Jnr Ltd and took possession of the assets. The cottages of Upper Wood and Middle Row were transferred to Robert Bingham in 1943. The passage of the assets of the mill into the ownership of The Stanton Estate Company, while unfortunate for the company, provided access to the funds of its major creditor, giving it the help it needed during the depression. Thus the mill was able to reopen and continue to employ the people in the village with Mr Humphrey Davie-Thornhill of the

Cressbrook in the early 1900s

Stanton Estate Company taking a place on the company board and the Dickies and Mallisons continuing the day-to-day management of the mill. Mr Humphrey Davie-Thornhill and Peter Dickie, Matthew Dickie's son, played particularly important roles during this time and worked extremely hard to keep the mill solvent with Mr Davie-Thornhill managing the mills finances and the operation of the company board.

Also surrendered to the creditors at this time were both Cressbrook Hall and Ravenstor House, although Cressbrook Hall was quickly sold on and subsequently let to the Columbia Picture Company who used it as an out-of-London headquarters during the Second World War. The Hall later passed through several more ownerships and spent time as a stud, a

pig farm and as a convent before being acquired in 1979 by the Hull-Bailey family, who continue to live there. Having survived the worst of the depression years by sacrificing the assets of the estate of Cressbrook, the mill operated in a state of measured decline for the next thirty years. In a effort to make it more efficient, one of the actions taken was to switch the

mill from self-generated electricity to a supply bought in from a commercial electricity generator. So it was in the mid-1950s that the mill started taking electricity from the newly nationalised Midlands Electricity Company. The on-site steam turbines shut down for good and the houses of the village started to receive a commercial electricity supply.

Cressbrook Mill's isolation and high running costs together with increased and cheaper thread production in the far-east steadily encroached on its markets and with order books running down irretrievably, the mill finally ceased operating as a going concern in 1965. As a producer at the luxury end of the thread market, Cressbrook Mill inevitably suffered earlier than other mills whose stock-in-trade was standard threads. These mills continued to operate for some time after Cressbrook Mill's demise.

The final page in the mill order book

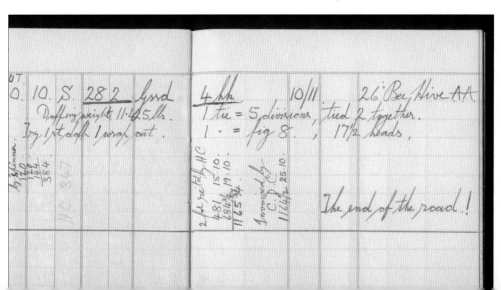

CENSUS REPORTS FROM 1901

The records of 1901 bring us now into what is living memory. The village was fully occupied and so we can assume the mill and the majority of residents still worked there. There had obviously been recruitment from other cotton towns as well over half of the 'incomers' had come from Lancashire, Cheshire, Yorkshire or Derby itself and only a minority came from local villages. Mrs Elizabeth Walker who was probably the last of the Duke of York's school apprentices was still a farmer and her daughter Margaret and husband Robert Smith ran the shop with the help of their son Henry. They had met when they were both in service at the Hall as lady's maid and butler respectively. John Burton a lead miner and his wife Hannah were in the Chapel House with their three younger children and four grandchildren, two of whom were already working at the Mill. On Top Row, Isaac Goodman was established as a mineral water manufacturer. The glass bottles he used, with their distinctive glass marble in the neck, have been found in the village. Also in Top Row was Josiah Alsop a greengrocer. There were three Ponsonby families in the village, that of Harry Ponsonby is of particular interest as we remember Richard, who was then only three.

REMEMBER WHEN...

From another generation: past and present inhabitants of Cressbrook recall vividly their adventures as both children and as grown-ups

MIRIAM & GORDON SHARPLEY

DANCING

Miriam: When we first started courting I was nineteen, Gordon was seventeen, a toyboy. We met down at Masson Mill at Matlock Bath, that's the first time we went out and we used to go to Buxton Pavilion Gardens a lot. But Gordon used to go off with the boys boozing till I got into the club in the Pavilion Gardens so I paid for myself, he didn't have to pay for me.
Gordon: It was because I couldn't afford to. I started driving for

In 1971, Amanda Bingham, Mandy Gratton and Jackie Sharpley danced safely in the streets with few cars around, watched by Louie the dog

Andrew's Coaches and I was the driver that used to take them to the dances in the finish. We used to start off in Cressbrook and then go to Litton Mill and Millers Dale then Tideswell if there was any from Tideswell. Well it started off when I was seventeen with the minibus, well like an eight-seater taxi and I used to try and pick Miriam up down at Litton Mill. People used to pay for this service to take them to the dance, so on a Saturday night they used to start off and sometimes there was as many as thirty people from round the area. But I mean you're going back to the Joe Loss, Ted Heath bands, you know the big bands. And Cyril Stapleton, Acker Bilk all them sort of people all used to come to the Pavilion Gardens and so Saturday night was the night.

THE PICTURES

Gordon: We'd got a cinema at Tideswell, we'd got a cinema at Bakewell and Saturday nights five o'clock, I think it was five o'clock, North Western Bus used to come from Matlock and it used to come right round all round the villages. Tideswell, Litton, come down into Cressbrook, start at the mill five o'clock and work its way up and by the time it got to Litton sometimes it was packed, the bus was full, taking people to the pictures, either Tideswell or Bakewell. Then it used to return back into Tideswell at nine fifteen and there was just a mad scramble and very often people were stood up coming back to Litton and Cressbrook. I know they always say they was never good old days, but to

me they were good old days, I used to enjoy it. I know we're getting on in life a bit but I mean it was a big thing to go to the cinema, we used to call it the pictures in them days, but it was a lovely thing. There was never any trouble, you didn't go with your parents, very rare your parents went.
Miriam: We used to pay seven pennies then and you used to be sat on forms in the front row and then when the lights went out we used to sneak back to the back, to the good seats which was about one and six. Up in the balcony it was about one and nine. But then the usherette, whatever you called her, used to come round and usher you back to your seats. It was fun, I mean it wasn't malicious or anything.
Gordon: We used to all get to the gates, big iron gates where you went up these steps to the cinema at Tideswell and when you think about it now you laugh. We'd all be there and you were clung to the gates and it must have been 20, 30 deep sometimes waiting for these gates opening. Jack Dean he was called and he used to come down with a key and he used to come down very proud you know, down all these steps and he'd open the gate and he'd hardly time to take the lock off and he was very near flattened up against the wall, everyone was through and it was straight up the

'Excuse me, can we borrow your bike?' That's how it was in the village

steps to see who could get to pay first to go in. It was quite a laugh 'cos there's this bloke pinned back against the wall. If you were noisy or you caused a disturbance they threw you out. They'd come round with the torch you know, told you to be quiet and if you weren't they threw you out. The film was very often breaking down and of course everybody would start shouting and jeering and all this sort of thing. And then when it came back on again they cheered but as soon as it had finished about half eight, something like that, everybody knew the routine. It was down to the chip shop, get a bag of chips and then it was nearly bus time. Very often you were half way up the village and you could hear voices all over the place, 'bus is coming, bus is coming,' you

know top of their voice and you had to run and the trouble was if you missed the bus you had to walk home. No taxis or minicabs, you couldn't afford anything like that, so it was walk home on the roads but you didn't think anything of it. If we went to Bakewell, it was a bit more modern Bakewell Cinema, and the latest bus back to this village was I think, eight thirty or quarter to nine. So if you missed that, the next bus only brought you to Ashford so you had to walk from Ashford to Cressbrook. We used to do that on a regular basis, never used to think anything about it. Sometimes we'd take our pushbikes up to Monsal Head and then all we did was walk from Ashford to Monsal Head and then bike. But in them days we didn't all have bikes, so we used to have to go around the village borrowing bikes 'Excuse me, can we borrow your bike?' That's how it was in the village.

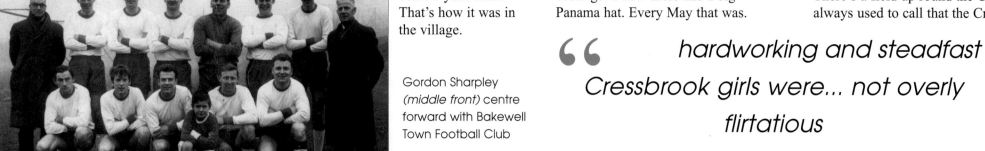

Gordon Sharpley (*middle front*) centre forward with Bakewell Town Football Club

VERA MUNNS

This was the first village that had electricity and the water supply was wonderful, we were only talking about this the other day, about the water that was pumped up from the private well, spring water, wonderful. As was the water at Ravensdale 'cos the well down there was the only supply we had when we lived down there. The waters a rival to Buxton but we thought it was better tasting, Buxton's a funny taste. Ken used to make his beer with it didn't you? He used to go down and fetch water from there to make his homebrew.

We had a Sunday School at Church and Chapel as well then and we had concerts at the Chapel, people from far away used to come and give concerts and then we used to go to them. On Chapel Anniversary a band used to go round and stop at different places and play for us. The Sunday School Anniversary was another time you could get a new dress and a big Panama hat. Every May that was.

Vera Munns (Ponsonby)

Oh we never used to walk out on a Sunday without a hat and gloves, we used to go to Chapel, morning, afternoon and evening service and we used to have a walk up to Monsal Head every Sunday, we always wore hats and gloves, every Sunday. And now it's all haphazard isn't it, nobody bothers, Sunday's no different to any other day.

There wasn't the traffic then and we used to play on the street you see so you could play cricket and all sorts on the road, sit outside the club with a bottle of pop and a bag of crisps and that was as far as your spending money went.

There's a photograph of a women's football team in the club - that's before my time, there's nobody left on that photograph now. Ken's auntie Mary used to play in it and my Auntie, two of my aunties. The goalie used to live at Rock House, Mrs Bennet. She was Clara Smith then but on the photograph she was Mrs Bennet, big hefty woman. There's a field up round the Church we always used to call that the Cricket

"hardworking and steadfast Cressbrook girls were... not overly flirtatious"

Edward Sheldon and Mr Savage, the headmaster at the primary school, keep the Cressbrook Ladies Football Team in order

Field, we used to have all our galas up there, every year.
We used to play whist at home, snakes and ladders and ludo, that's what we did in our spare time and listen to the radio. We always had the radio 'cos my Dad built the first radio in the village. He sent away for all the parts and my Dad used to sit with the head phones on and every time my Mum stepped out they used to say 'Is it right your Tom's built a radio?' They was clever you see in their own way they were, they could do anything.

Ken came from Derby - I'd known of him for ages. He came up first on holiday when he was nine, came on holiday down Monsal Dale, the bug of Cressbrook bit him and after he came out of the Navy he came marching up here. I'll tell you something else in a

minute, we've been talking about this the last week or two. If ever a man came up or a boy came up to the village to see a girl he never went back single, from anywhere. It's true, I'm going to make a record of it, a written record of who came and who never went back, funny it's in my mind at present. I'm about to make a list and I'll show you it one day, right back to Joan Thorpe's father-in-law's days, he came up from Ashford. There were four particular boys they came camping, they always had the Whit Field, it's a nickname you know of Ravensdale Field, that flat field near the brook, cos of the water there. Don't know if it was five or six of them, and all married Cressbrook girls and they came from Barnsley and Mexborough area. Steadfast I would think, that's what was special about the Cressbrook girls. Hardworking and steadfast Cressbrook girls were, not overly flirtatious.

A Sunday School outing in Cressbrook

We went dancing you know in our teens, we used to walk to Ashford and Bakewell and dance all night and then walk back again, safely. Well, it's not as safe now is it for youngsters? I mean we went out more or less as soon as we left school and never used to think anything of it. The dances had to be over at quarter to twelve because it was Sunday the next day, that's another standard that's gone. We used to go and catch the train at Millers Dale and go down to Buxton, the Pavilion Gardens, where all the big bands came, Geraldo and Joe Loss. Ashford dances they were just like a hop. I think it was one and six to go in, a threepenny hop sort of thing. They used to put the table up in the interval and you used to have a sandwich or a bun and a cup of tea, down it went and you were dancing again. I used to think Ashford Institute was massive and I go in now and it's like somebody's parlour. I wonder how we ever danced in there you know, but it was lovely.
Cressbrook Hall it was too staid, we weren't allowed to go to Cressbrook Hall, we could never go in any part but the stables. We had a bun fight there once a year where Hetty lives now, that used to be all open, what they called the stables - they had horses - but oh no you were never allowed to go down to the Hall.
I want to live to be 100 mind you, then drop dead. I'm no trouble to anybody and I want to live to be 100 because I might miss something that's going on.

"Don't panic". In May 1940 Anthony Eden, Secretary of State for War, appealed for recruits to join the Local Defence Volunteers the LDV, also known as Look, Duck and Vanish. At first the recruits were mainly ex-servicemen from the First World War and gradually more men joined from the reserved professions (ie teachers). Within 6 weeks of the announcement there were 200,000 volunteers, swelling to 1.8million by 1943. In July, when the long awaited uniforms and weapons arrived, Winston Churchill changed the name to the Home Guard. In November 1944 the Home Guard was stood down and on December 31 1945 was formally disbanded.

above: the Home Guard marching through Tideswell crossroads

VE Day: 8th May 1945 residents of Cressbrook celebrating the event

PAT KELLY

We older children were allowed to go to the cinema in Tideswell on Saturday nights. It was a $4\frac{1}{2}$ mile walk and the films were ancient, shown in a village hall. About seven of us used to go and then when the film was over we bought fish and chips for the long walk home. Between Litton and Cressbrook is the graveyard behind a low dry-stone wall. We always felt it was a ghostly place and used to run like mad past it. One night was very eerie as the moon was very bright and occasionally went behind a cloud. Peggy and I had dawdled and got behind the others when we got to the spot where we felt particularly nervous so we held hands and ran past the graveyard.

Suddenly we heard this terrible noise and saw something huge and white as the moon reappeared, and stones started falling down from the wall. We ran so fast our hearts nearly gave out. Then when we looked behind us we saw in the bright moonlight that it was a white horse that had reared against the wall and had started whinnying with fright after we disturbed it. We never dawdled after that!

London was now getting the doodlebugs and Columbia Pictures had hired Cressbrook Hall to house the wives and children of their employees for the duration of the war. This was a great opportunity for Doris and Mum who fixed up a room at the Lodge as a hairdressing salon. The Columbia wives were very trendy Londoners and soon Mum and Doris were making a lot of money over their weekend visits before returning to the salon in Manchester for weekdays.

The London children had a bad time with the village children, in fact nearly the whole Columbia entourage decided that they would rather face death in the bombing than exist in Cressbrook! Most went back fairly soon so Mum and Doris's fortunes were fairly short lived.

We had no electricity, an outside loo, no radio, no cooker, no bathroom and I was used to luxury so it was almost like camping! Mrs Lomas cooked delicious meals on a primus stove or in the oven next to the fire and my bath - once a week - was in the tin bath in front of the fire. The hot water was ladled out of a black tank next to the fire. No tap water - just a pump in the kitchen for cold water. This was all very exciting to me and I loved the woods around the cottage, the wonderful country smells and scenery. I made two friends, Peggy Walker and Margery Smith, both my age and nicer than the city girls.

ISOBEL SUTCLIFFE

I lived at School House and I was born there in the sitting room, the far room and my father was the engineer at the mill. He'd worked at the mill and when the Great War came he had to go to Manchester where he worked on munitions for a Dutch firm called Hans Renolds and he also made chains for prisoners. There he met my mother and they got married and came back to Cressbrook. I was the second child and I had an older sister called Mary and we both went to Cressbrook School next door. The house belonged to the mill, all the property did. I don't know whether they paid any rent or if they lived rent free. I never saw any rent book so they perhaps lived rent free I don't know, perhaps it went with his job. I worked in the office at the mill and started there when I was probably about 14 or 15, well it was before Mum died of course and Mary worked in the bottle winding. I got married in 1943 and my husband was in the Air Force, he went to India for 3

Isobel Swindell (Sutcliffe)

Mr and Mrs Swindell, Isobel's parents

years. When he came home in 1946 I left the office and I didn't go to work anymore, I looked after the house.

When I was little we used to have the dustcart down what I call the backs where I lived at School House. They used to have ashpits there and you used to put your cinders in and the toilets were there as well, there were eight toilets I think. When you went to the toilet it used to drop into the ashpits along with the cinders and all the tins and all the rubbish and then the dustman used to come with the horse and cart and he used to have to jump in and shovel it out, put it in the cart and take it away, so that wasn't very hygienic. We had a pan toilet in the yard near the gate and he used to empty that and put it into the cart. The horse was called Captain and mother used to make him oatmeal in an enamel bowl, mixed it with water and he used to love that. He used to suck it up and then he used to get the bowl in his mouth and throw it up in the air and all the enamel had come off all the way round where he'd had his teeth on it. She made it for him every week. Captain collapsed and died on the station hill going for coal. There was a pump house and that was to do with drinking water up in the

village and I used to go with my dad and he'd have to oil it. I can smell it now, it had a certain smell the oil in there and it used to squelch up and down in those things and I wouldn't be very old and he used to say 'Stay there' and he would go across to where there was a wheel in the river. And he used to get a little ladder and go down out of sight, and I used to stand and think what if he doesn't come up because the river would be flowing fast. I watched for his cap, he used to wear a cap, and if I could see his cap coming up I knew he was ok. Then we'd walk back home and we used to do that every Sunday, walk there and oil the pump that would pump water up to the village, up to that tank in the stone pit I told you about. I don't know where the water came from, there must have been a spring there that came down the wood, but that was very often our Sunday afternoons. I remember it was so cold one Christmas morning

> ## " I watched for his cap, he used to wear a cap, and if I could see his cap coming up I knew he was OK "

when I was living at the School House, that it froze the saliva in the band instruments and we had to bring them in and put them in front of the fire before they could play. I always made the bandsmen rum and coffee on Christmas morning when they came, you know, and we had a postman in those days who came on Christmas Day and he came from Millers Dale on his bike. He had whiskers and looked like Father Christmas. We always had a post on Christmas Day and sometimes he got a little merry and one Christmas morning my dad

Fred Worsencroft and Bill Swindell repairing the wall in the Goyt on a home-made raft

found his bag with the letters in it and he had to take it to where he lived in Millers Dale. He used to get a drink at the houses on Christmas morning and I guess it would be sherry in one house and whisky in another. Mr Kyme he was called. But it made your Christmas cards seem different when he brought them 'cos he was like Santa, he was a lovely man.

I used to go to the pictures with my friend Olive. We used to walk from Cressbrook Mill, we worked in the office and we used to leave there when we'd finished and walk to Millers Dale to catch the train to Buxton and then we used to have to come out sometimes before the picture was over to catch the train back. Mr Dickie used to laugh and to say 'One of these days you'll miss the train.' He used to go on his bike in war time 'cos he couldn't get the petrol and we had to run sometimes to get back. Olive didn't go to dances, I used to go to the pictures with her but I used to go with other girls from the village to dances and we could share a taxi back. Sometimes we could go to Tideswell pictures and I used to go with Olive. She lived at the top of the village on Lower Wood so I used to have to walk down from there by myself and I used to keep shouting to her until she was out of hearing you know. Then I used to run all the way down the hill and there'd only be a cow coughing or something in the field to frighten you nothing else to worry about in those days not like it is today, it's like a different world isn't it?

MARGERY HOYLE

I was born in Monsal Dale in 1926 and I was there 'til I was 12 years old when we moved away to a larger farm in a little village on the borders of Cheshire and Derbyshire. I went to Cressbrook school from the age of five till the age of 12 and I had two brothers Sam and Bob and four sisters, twins who are next to me and there was five years between the twins and myself so I was the youngest. My sisters, Kathleen, Dorothy, Betty and Nora - our maiden name was Furniss - worked in Cressbrook in the cotton mill and it was quite hard work I believe, I never had to do that because I was the youngest. My sisters at the weekends used to go dancing down in Longstone or Bakewell, having to walk rather a long way. We all had to walk to school because there were no buses or anything in the village. We had a good life really, we hadn't any money at all, my mother used to do teas, she used to take in lodgers and she used to get a lot of hikers from Sheffield come down 'cos they thought Monsal Dale was so beautiful which it is. My eldest sister thought it was awful because she just said it was all hard work and that's all she ever remembered about it you know, helping with the teas, helping with lodgers and having to go out to work

An early view of the River Wye showing the stepping stones, footbridge and ford

Upperdale's spectacular position

as well, but as a child I thought it was good you know. There were teas for the hikers, teas for any visitors that came, people would stop in the Dale and you know just come in and have pots of tea and yes, it was hard work but it was all helping to keep the family going really. Mother was a hard worker, considering she hadn't been brought up to farm life. She used to make all her own bread and any animal my father killed of course everything had to be used. He used to kill pigs and things like that which I hated. I used to run away and hide when they killed the pigs 'cos they squealed so much you know. But being a butcher he knew how to do all the meat cuts and my mother made black puddings and pies.

I don't really remember the lodgers. I think that was more or less before I was born. But I know that they did have the odd lodgers you know, probably only temporary it wouldn't be for any length of time probably

somebody waiting to move. The Sheffield hikers and bikers and cyclists, they used to come and they'd camp in one of the fields at the bottom of the road but also when it was bad weather in winter they still wanted to come, so my father used to let them sleep in the barns. They didn't mind, they thought it was lovely, washing in the well outside or wash in the river. We got to know them quite well you know, in fact I think one or two of the Sheffield lads married Cressbrook girls because they came so often. I think there were one or two romances made when they used to come over. We used to get people on the trains - well before the cars - and people used to walk or they'd walk down from Monsal Head, perhaps parking their cars at the top and walk down and of course then there was the Warren down where the waterfall is.

Living next to the river was lovely as long as you didn't go near the very deep part, which was twenty feet deep just in front of the house. In actual fact it was a wonder my mother didn't have a heart attack every time we went out anywhere near the river but I suppose she got used to it. We knew

I just slipped off a log and fell in face first with all my clothes on

where we could paddle, my sisters learned to swim and my brother learned to swim in the river but I didn't, I was always terrified of water. I nearly drowned once that was why, well I thought I'd nearly drowned. I mean I was quite convinced I'd drowned in the river. We were playing there but it wasn't in a very deep part and I just slipped off a log and fell in face first with all my clothes on and my brother dragged me out and took me home. I wasn't happy with water and I've never liked it since although I have learned to swim but I'm not very good. I was only about four or five something like that, but it sticks in your mind.

BRIAN BINGHAM

Cressbrook Club was built as a village institute on the understanding at the time I think from what I've been told, I've never actually seen it in writing on the understanding that it never held a license for alcohol. I believe it was pretty well patronised before the war, with a billiard table in the main club room and there was a reading room, and I think that's about it really. Probably dominoes and darts and then it closed during the war. In actual fact I was instrumental in getting it opened again. When I was 13 years old I'd seen this building - I'd actually been in, because Tony Bingham's father actually lived in the flat below the club so I used to go in with Tony while the place was closed and it was actually Tony that taught me to play snooker upstairs on the snooker table. But as I say I'd seen it closed and I knew it was owned by a bloke called Humphrey Davy of Davy Estates. So I wrote to him when I was thirteen to ask him if we could open a youth club in the village institute and I never got a reply from him but he got in touch with Ernest Bingham, that was Tony's father who lived there, who got in touch with one or two more blokes in the village at that

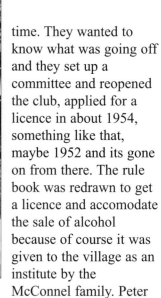

time. They wanted to know what was going off and they set up a committee and reopened the club, applied for a licence in about 1954, something like that, maybe 1952 and its gone on from there. The rule book was redrawn to get a licence and accomodate the sale of alcohol because of course it was given to the village as an institute by the McConnel family. Peter Willis, who used to be the milkman round our way, was treasurer and I was secretary and at that time the place was different. It was a large vaulted roof and I mean it was very high, the toilets were outside, in fact the gents was just out in the corner there, it'd no roof on at all so if it was raining then you got wet. The ladies was across in the outbuildings and the only door was at the east end. So Peter and myself and the rest of the committee set to and we managed to get the bar moved from where it was, up by what used to be the reading room, up at the top end and put toilets inside, put a front door in and so on and so forth, so we were quite pleased with ourselves at that time because we were only in our twenties and it's sort of gone on ever since.

> " *it'd no roof on, so if it was raining you got wet* "

TWO LIVES

Paul Dickie and Arthur Barnes talk about their lives in Cressbrook and at the mill where they worked together for many years

Paul Dickie in Royal Marines uniform in 1939

PAUL DICKIE

My father I think was born at Litton Mill in the house opposite Litton Mill and he went to Tideswell Grammar School. He went on from there to Rossall School which I believe is somewhere near Blackpool and he joined the mill when he was 18. Now he was born in 1890 'cos he was 30 when I was born in 1920, so he started at the mill as soon as he'd finished going to school at Rossall. My father lived in Cressbrook and I was born in Rock House but we moved to Buxton when I was about ten months old. My grandfather lived in Mill House which is opposite Litton Mill and the story is rather interesting. After a while my grandmother on my father's side, Mrs Dickie, said to her husband 'I'm not living in this pokey mill house anymore I'd like a nice house to live in.' So they had Ravenstor built in the early 1900s. My grandfather had a friend who lived in Bakewell who was an architect and he asked him to design the house. The architect, being no fool, realised that the site at Ravenstor was easily seen from the main LMS railway and thought 'what a wonderful advert.' So he built, he designed this house which was much bigger than grandfather really wanted it, so the story goes. My grandfather took a partner called Mr Mallison and Mr Mallison and his wife eventually bought Cressbrook Hall. Ravenstor is where I spent nearly all my childhood and school holidays. I very much regret that I didn't find out a lot more about Tiad Dickie because Tiad is Welsh for grandfather and my mother was one of three sisters from a Mrs Stanley who was Welsh, so we always called grandfather Tiad and Grandmother Nian but I've often regretted I didn't find out more about him. I've got photographs of he and I together in the garden in Ravenstor. It's a youth hostel now and I let them have a lot of photographs about two years ago in which I am there with Tiad Dickie and my sister. They're in what they called the drawing room. But if you go to Ravenstor and ask if you can look at the photographs they've written some kind of script alongside the pictures. Ravenstor when I was a little boy was in wonderful condition. I remember in those days there was two housemaids and a cook, a head gardener, three under-gardeners and a chauffeur... some money around in those days. I only went to Cressbrook Hall once or twice 'cos Mr Mallison, who owned Cressbrook Hall, had married a Belgian lady and she used to have some of her nieces and nephews come to stay and we used to go for tea sometimes and play. I haven't been there since I was about 14 or 15.

I was in the services during the war in the Royal Marines. I joined up in 1937 and then of course we were called up in 1939 and when I came out of the services I was 26 and my father had always been looking forward to having me come into the mill, so when I was demobbed in January '46 and I

Ravenstor House, now a youth hostel

joined him within two months. My first role at the mill was really to learn how the mill worked as I'd no knowledge of cotton or cotton trade or machinery or anything: so I just had to learn what each department did and how the machinery worked.

I was living in Buxton, so father and I used to drive down. Well first of all, when I joined the firm in 1946, we didn't have a car so we used to catch the little push and pull train from Buxton to Millers Dale and we actually had a cycle, very nice ride down. We called it the push and pull because there was one engine you see and there was no turning ring so if the engine was in the front it pulled down to Millers Dale and then it pushed the little carriage back, so it was called the push and pull. But my father, during the war, he didn't have a bicycle and he used to walk every day from Millers Dale station to Cressbrook Mill and back again at night - in the dark in winter and by the river which could be a little bit dangerous.

There wasn't a vast turnover in staff, there was a certain amount of turnover of course when some of the younger girls were pregnant and some of the older ladies decided they'd had enough, but it was a very happy family mill, a lot of singing all the time, especially in the cop-winding they

used to sing all the songs that we sang during the war, 'Roll out the barrel' and those sort of things, it was a very happy atmosphere, yes.

I persuaded my father we ought to have a works outing and we went to Blackpool. Well I must have heard that mills had works outings, so I thought well its time we had one at our mill, so that was the main reason. I think Blackpool was the first one which was a great success and then we had three or four more after that until short time started to hit in the mill and then we couldn't

afford it. We certainly provided the bus but I don't remember giving them spending money but if Arthur says so ... I don't remember me father ever giving me spending money.

There was no canteen area there, there was a sort of heating stove. The workers used to bring their meals and if it was a hot meal they would put it in a big oven which was there and they'd heat it up ready for their lunch. Well the workers were very self-sufficient

and we didn't do anything, father and I. We used to take sandwiches down in a little tin box each for our lunch. There was no pension scheme at all, we didn't have a pension scheme, which in this day and age would be dreadful wouldn't it? So these poor people, I mean when they retired, they had to retire on what they could afford to save and when I started to work at the mill, a man's full wage for working in the doubling room, they were the highest paid people, was about six pounds a week,

Usually if you came into the mill you started as a doffer, that was the people who took the full bobbins of yarn from the doubling room off their spindles and put them in a skip. There'd be about five or six doffer's I think. Arthur started off as a doffer, so he would maybe tell you more about it than I know. Some of the doffers were girls.

> ## *They had some pretty girls too in the bobbin winding room... some from Cressbrook, some from Litton*

back row: Sheila Howe, Miriam Sharpley, Dorothy Gregory, Bertie Redfern *front row:* Wendy Mulling, Sylvia Hambleton, Maggie McKone, Debra Ponsonby, Maggie Ponsonby, Dorothy Walker

43

Paul Dickie and
Arthur Barnes

From there, if there was a vacancy in either the cop winding room or the bobbin winding room, we would ask if any of them wanted to learn bobbin or cop winding if they were going to stay, ladies do that work. They had some pretty girls too in the bobbin winding room. Some from Cressbrook some from Litton, yes I won't mention names. Arthur may have mentioned them. The men never did cop or bobbin winding, they would either go into the doubling room and obviously they'd opt for the doubling room because the gassing room wasn't very well ventilated. I mean the poor men, their faces were black with gassing fumes and being not used to working in a gassing room you couldn't stay in

there more than 10 minutes, it was dreadful, absolutely dreadful. Did no good whatever to your lungs, terrible. I don't think Arthur ever worked in the gassing room, he'd more sense.
The development of the mill is wonderful, it was so distressing to see it when it was falling to bits. I remember it for all the humming machinery and the singing, the girls singing and to see it sort of falling to bits was dreadful. But I think they've done a wonderful job in fact they've done a wonderful job on both mills. I didn't know they'd done Litton Mill until somebody told me so I had a drive down there and I was surprised to see how nice that looked too. There is a steep road opposite Litton Mill

and when I was a little boy they used to have motor-cycle trials seeing if the motor-cycles could get up the hill, that was fun to watch.
For the first 15 years after the war, the mill prospered. We were doing very well and then the Far East learned how to build humidifiers and of course you need a damp atmosphere for cotton to really gel together, so a lot of the trade was taken by the Far East. We had short time and the mill was shut for two days in a week and then three days in a week and so we finally had to close it down in 1966 I think it was. That was very sad having had the business for nearly a hundred years as a family business. "

" **ARTHUR BARNES**
I was originally born in Sheffield and we came here from Longstone. Well, me mum and dad, we were Salvation Armyists and we lived in Sheffield and they wanted to come out into country and they saw this advert for cottage in Longstone, so they came and had a look at it and of course they jumped at it, rent three and three a week - I'll let you work that out. I worked with this plumber from when I was about ten year old at weekend and the arrangement with this plumber was that if I signed indentures he would make the business out to me when he died. Then me mam went and got TB and she had to go into hospital and I had to find another job because I forget how much it was, only about six pence an hour or something like that, I had to get more money, so that's when I came here to the mill. I was 14. Well, me dad only had one leg and he's a bad arm, he'd got a leg off in 1914 war and his pension to start with was 24 shilling a week. They got married, it was still 24 shilling a week. I came along, still 24 shilling a week and then me sisters came along, two sisters, still 24 shilling a week and it wasn't until the Labour government got in in 1945 that it went up to £6 odd, me dad's pension. Yes, and I always remember me dad sat there and he said 'You know I've never been as rich in my life', that was £6 week.
That's how I came here in '41, during the war. You had to start at the

On duty. Arthur Barnes in Fleet Air Arm uniform

beginning, sweeping up and things like that and then gradually trained going through the mill. Then I went into Fleet Air Arm and when I came out I got a letter. They weren't going to set me on again. I said, 'You've got to start me it's the rule you know in forces.' 'Yes, we know that, we'll write you a letter and explain what we want you to do.' Mr Swindell was the chief engineer and I'd be working under Mr Swindell and if I behaved myself, cos I was a bit of a rogue, he says 'We'll take you on and you'll have a more interesting job.' He were understanding, Mr Swindell. That's how I got to be on the engineering side, I learned it from him. I tackled things then that I would never tackle now, putting these big shafts, six-inch shafts in the machines. If it breaks, get lorry, take the old shaft to somewhere up near Manchester - pick it up next day - it were hard work. There were about a 180 people, something like that, were working at the mill after the war and they came

Well, after the war when you were grown up, could put it this way, on a grown up job, about three pound something a week

from Ashford, Bakewell. Bus came up, North Western it was then. It was the mill that ran it in a way, but it were a service bus. Half past seven it came and came at 5 o'clock at night to pick up again. Half past seven I think it was till about five, it was a long day, very interesting though, and that's how I started there. I always remember when

far right: William Swindell chief engineer at Cressbook Mill

war was going to finish. We were putting new shafts, about five of us, where the water wheel is up the road, pumping water up the river, below the Hall. There was a pump house there, they used to pump the water up to tanks in the village, so that was our water. That was the drinking water, beautiful water, but it was very hard so

everybody had a tank either at back of house and caught water off the roof 'cos that was soft and they used to do the washing with that, but what was interesting about that was the manager says, 'Now we think the war is going to finish today.' So he says 'As soon as I get to know, I'll send our Isobel up and I want you to finish straight away, come down and we'll have a little chat and a drink and that's it'. Of course Isobel came up, I'd say it was about 11 o'clock: 'War's over now'. The old engineer wouldn't go down, of course us young uns we wanted to start bending our elbows but no we had to wait till 5 o'clock. We had to finish job off as the mill used to look after the water, make sure the water's OK.

It was very awkward 'cos I was working with old Billy, grand old bloke he was, very clever and I thought, well it's a bit awkward this to know that you're taking his job over when he finishes. Then I were working with him one day and tears were streaming down his face and I said 'What's up Mr Swindell?' He said 'They've sacked me.' I knew what was going off, so I had to be careful what I said, I said 'What do you mean sacked?' He says, 'Oh they've sacked me'. But what had happened, they were changing over from steam turbine to mains electric and electric motors and he wouldn't have it. He said 'No I'm not having it.' He said 'I'm keeping this steam turbine.' When boss says 'I don't want you to

45

finish but you'll have to finish' 'cos he didn't think he'd take him up on that. Billy said 'That's what I'll do, I'll finish.' So he finished. I'm guessing now it was '55 something like that. Electric's less work and cheaper to run. To have a steam turbine you had big chimneys with coal fires. Anybody

ran the coal fire but I'd do it sometimes and we used to get the coal which came at the beginning to Monsal Dale station and it used to be one of my jobs to go with wagon. I used to go and get, I think about three ton in this wagon, used to bring two loads in a morning. Hand-shovelling it

> *there were a bloke used to drive wagon then, called John Bond and he was as crafty as a cart-load of monkeys*

Arthur takes part in a protest in the 1970s against the state of the mill and its general neglect

out of wagons, best part about it, there were a bloke used to drive wagon then called John Bond and he was as crafty as a cart-load of monkeys. I was a silly beggar, I used to go down there, a young lad like, I'll show you I can fill this wagon up, 'I'll have to go to toilet' he'd say. And you could see him poking his head over wall seeing if I'd filled wagon up yet. Silly beggar me, I used to fill wagon up. Depended whether it was summer or winter, you had to go more in winter time because the mill was warmed by steam pipes, in summer it didn't matter and then every so often every year, they used to have what they call a shutdown. We used to work holidays and have our holidays later on and try and get about half a dozen people, young uns or people who were useful and strong. Strong to fill boilers and clear boiler out and chip lime-stone off boiler. It was very interesting, actually.

In the summer if they could afford it they ran a mill trip to Blackpool. Sometimes we didn't work Saturdays, we went to Menai Bridge, Llandudno, Blackpool. They paid for the trip, they also treated you to dinner and I can't

remember whether they used to give us half-a-crown spending money, something like that. Manager's son used to come with us and he's a bit older than me and the bosses in the mill, they were the old type of bosses you respected em, and this boss's son got on table, at what they called half-way house - it were like where bus stopped half-way to give you a bit of a rest and that and have a drink, and he danced on table. 'Cos that was unheard of that, manager's son doing that. Well, what was strange, it's not all that long since, two year might be three, knock come at door, I went out there he says 'Don't you remember me?' I said 'No, I'm not very good at remembering faces.' He said 'I'm Paul Dickie' 'Oh' I said 'I can see you now dancing on table.' And that were it, we were on about this dancing on table. There was a trade union rep in the mill, I forgot what his name was, he wasn't much for workers. We put in for a rise and he came down to look at us and went into office, he used to go into office, have his drink and that's all he was really interested in 'cos later he popped his head in, 'I've got you that rise'. Oh thanks, ha'penny an hour, that's what he got us, there weren't discussions in them days. Well, after the war when you were grown up, could put it this way on a grown up job, about three pound something a week. But one thing about 'em, especially in gassing room, if say they were somebody short they'd say to people that worked there, now will you do that job between you, they gave you his wage. Nice place to work.

What they've done to the mill, they've made a very, very good job of it. I know people say, well they've spoiled the mill, but I mean we've been there since David bought it and we could imagine it falling down. Then Peak

Wye Mill during restoration

Park at one time, were going to buy it. We didn't particularly want them to buy it because we could imagine a nice big car park there with toilets and little shops, it wouldn't have been Cressbrook then. Then there was another bloke after it, Prince Charles. Prince Charles were after it, he wanted it for backwards children. Been down here once or twice looking at it. Yes, I like the new Mill building. I know people say there's going to be too many cars, but we haven't noticed that yet have we?

We know village is going to change, it has changed and it's the people that knew what the old village was like. It's a bit of a shame that its changed but its not all I want. Correspondent from Sheffield paper, I think it were

An illustration of the restored turbine machinery by Keith Hislop

Telegraph, she wrote an article about Cressbrook and she says in two or three years time it'll be a satellite town of Sheffield, Derby and that. She's quite right, it is. I mean I don't blame her thinking 'I'd like to live in Cressbrook.' You can't blame people for doing that but its spoiled the village. I mean people will say, 'Where did you say Mrs Brown lives?' Well I live here but I don't know a quarter of people in Cressbrook now.

Sadly, Arthur Barnes died on the 13th September 2005, before publication of this book

The mill process in 1946

By the post WW2 era, Cressbrook's production of cotton thread was highly efficient. The mill continued to supply top quality thread until the UK industry collapsed. Here is how the streamlined process worked

After Paul Dickie left the Royal Marines in 1946 he joined his father in the family business. At that time there were about 80 people working at Cressbrook Mill. And around 90% were engaged in the process of spun thread creation through managing the machines themselves. Other roles were three office staff and ancillary jobs such as lorry driving, engineering, maintenance and boiler-room work. At this time the workforce were mostly women, with just five men in the gassing room and 15 in the doubling room. Many of the staff lived in rented accommodation in the village with the others walking, cycling or arriving on the North Western Buses.

The working day was 7:30am to 5.00pm with an hours break for lunch, Monday to Friday and overtime on Saturday morning.

The raw material of the mill at this time was raw Eygptian and American cotton thread supplied by cotton spinning mills. Cressbrook Mill produced from this a variety of finished cotton threads which were used in the manufacturing of woven cotton cloth.

1 The raw cotton thread arrived at the mill by lorry.

2 This floor, called 'Number 4', was where the incoming material was stored before going to cop winding.

3 The first process in the mill was called cop winding. In this, strands of thread from a number of cops were wound together onto a further spool. This room had six or seven machines with four people per machine.

4 The spools were then taken to the main doubling room where the machinery in the doubling room created the basic thread by twisting the threads together. This room had 20 machines and if fine yarn was being produced each person looked after two machines, but if coarser yarn was being made each person managed one and a half machines.

5 Little doubling room.

6 The reels of doubled thread were next taken to the bobbin winding room where the large quantities of thread were wound onto smaller bobbins to make them more manageable in the onward processes. At this point the thread was in a usable form and many cloth types could be made with it. However, finer quality cloth types required an extra process to remove the fluff from the surface of the thread caused by wayward cotton fibres. 75% of thread production at Cressbrook Mill was for this smoother, very high quality thread.

7 Then the threads went to the gassing room where the threads were rewound again, but during this time they were passed over a naked flame. The speed of the thread passing through the flame was sufficient to avoid the thread burning through, but enough to burn off excess fibres.

8 The final process for either gassed or ungassed thread was to wind it in the reeling room into large skeins or hanks, which weighed about two or three pounds each. The skeins or hanks were packed into crates for transport to the weavers. To save space they were pressed together so that eventually they formed what was virtually almost a solid block of cotton thread that had to be unpacked at the weaving mills before it could be woven.

9 Fine yarns with more than 300 threads were wound onto either beams or warps, in the beaming and warping room, and then moved to the warehouse in the basement of Wye Mill, prior to onward transport.

Crates of thread would be taken by lorry from Cressbrook to the company warehouse in Manchester two or three times a week for the weaving mills to collect. The Cressbrook lorries brought by return, more raw cotton thread and the process would start again. Around about this time Cressbrook sourced its raw cotton thread from six or seven different suppliers.
Cressbrook finished thread was sold predominantly to mills in Lancashire for the top end of the woven cotton market making poplin fabric.

Aerial view of Cressbrook Mill in 1946

The mill clock & gas house

For apprentices, mill-workers, villagers and now tourists, the clock has been a visual landmark for 168 years

CRESSBROOK MILL CLOCK HISTORY

Cressbrook Mill clock was installed in 1837 to commemorate the coronation of Queen Victoria and worked until the early 1970s when vandals stole some of the brass cogs and bearings. Whitehurst of London supplied the clock and only four of that type remain in the country today. The firm is now owned by Smiths of Derby and when they were contacted they knew immediately which clock it was and what it would need to start up again. The original workings are still in the roof eaves at Wye Mill. The three bells are in the cupola and the clock face and hands are still in situ. The clock could have been refurbished to be hand-wound and still ring the quarters and hours. But the new owners elected to have an electric motor version without chimes which automatically adjusts for British summer time and corrects itself after a power failure. The restoration cost £3000.

ISOBEL SUTCLIFFE

As a child you know it really was lovely living there, I've always got sort of happy memories of it. I used to 'fire up' if Dad was ill at the gas house. He suffered from bronchitis in the winter sometimes. The gas house has gone now, it was in the mill yard and they had a gasometer at the side and one room in the mill was the gassing room where the yarn went through a flame on the machinery, like a bunsen burner. And it went through the flame to get the fluff and things off and that's what they needed the gas for. If Dad wasn't well he used to say 'Can you go down and throw me some coke on' and I used to go and put it on the furnace, either 10 or 12 shovels I used to do. I was never frightened 'cos you weren't frightened in those days, there was no lights, there was only a little gas mantel on the wall and it was a huge furnace you know. I used to have to open the door with the shovel and then throw the coke on and then shut the door until the night watchman came. There was somebody on all night to keep the fire going because if the gasometer went down it would spoil the gas.

I used to wind the mill clock up as well. I think it was wound once a week but if Dad wasn't well he used to say 'Can you go?' It was right up on the top floor where the clock is now, well you walked in there, it was a very small room and there were holes in the floor, it was rotten a lot of the floor but I was used to it. I remember once when my husband was home Dad wasn't well and he said could I go and wind the clock up. It was when you had to alter it for the summer time or

The Mill Clock

Dear Folks,
I'd just like to remind you of how long I've been telling the time
It's from Victoria's Accession, with my two dials, as well as my chime.
In my young days I had lots of companions, the 'Apprentices' slept by my sides,
In their cubicles under the rafters they would hear me
when they opened their eyes.
Times have changed since they brought me from Derby,
with horses, a long way by road,
My maker was Whitehurst of Derby, who set me going in my lofty abode.
Mears, of London, cast my bells in the turret,
which I know you good folk like to hear,
They've been chiming there since my erection, day and night and year by year.
My former attendants have left me and passed on to where time is no more,
Yet I feel fit, in my prime, to keep going, and with many years still in store.
If they'll give me their kindly attention, my diallings and chimings are fine,
In 2000 I feel sure I'll be going, and ringing those good folks when to dine.

W.J. Swindell
January 1946

something, and he explained to Warren how to do it and when we got up there we'd forgotten and it struck 17 times! I remember all the people had come out of their houses because they wondered what was going wrong but that was the only occasion when we made a mistake. Dad was laughing when we got back - yes, he could hear it so he knew we'd done something wrong.

I know when we had anything special like Empire Day and things like that Dad used to put a flag up on the clock turret on the mill. He used to put a flag up there and I used to be a bit frightened of him falling off, but he used to go up with it. They don't perhaps do anything like that now but they used to on Empire Day or the King or Queen's birthday. I've got a letter here from Mr Dickie, its about the clock from the old mill so he must have put some money in for my Dad when he retired. Yes, it says

"Dear Mr Swindell,
thank you very much for putting my
liver, lights and other digestive organs
in order, nobody here understands how
I suffer in winter. Please accept the
enclosed as a token of my gratitude.
Your grateful patient,
Cressbrook Mill Clock

ARTHUR BARNES
When the clock started again, I'm glad I didn't have to go and wind it up. When it was the old mill clock it used to chime the quarters and the hours. It were alright until you wanted to go to sleep at about 12 o'clock at night. Yes, we used to have to wind it up twice a week and there were big heavy weights, silver weights on bank there. Now they probably weigh about three hundred weight, used to have to wind them from bottom to top and if you let them get too far down - they were cotton ropes ; originally I suppose they would be steel but they were cotton then and you know if you let them nearly to bottom then they'd twist and you'd have to unwind them. There's three bells there at the top in the cupola. They used to ring when the bell chimed to strike the quarters then the hours. One day manager says 'Oh good job for you Arthur' he says 'there's something wrong with that bell.' So I went up and had a look and bracket had broke for holding bell so it was tilted. He says 'Can you do anything with it?' I says, 'Get a car jack, jack it up and then re-bolt it.' Which is what we did.

left: Cressbrook Mill in 1907

right: The cupola and clock

Religious worship in Cressbrook

Unusually for a thriving rural community, there was no church in the village throughout the 19th century. With the arrival of Primitive Methodism in Cressbrook, this eventually lead to the building of Trinity Chapel

The fact that there was no place of formal worship in Cressbrook until 1902 makes it somewhat unusual. Society usually look after the needs of the soul ahead of any earthly needs and the church is often the oldest, best looked after and the most central of buildings in a village or town. Checks made by the Boards of Governers of the poorhouses from where many of the apprentices at Cressbrook Mill came ensured that the religious education of the children was looked after at the site, while the requirements of the adults were provided for by places of worship in the local villages. There were strong links at this time between Cressbrook Mill, Litton Mill and the church at Tideswell. It was only in 1844 that organised religion, in the form of Primitive Methodism, came to the community of Cressbrook. Methodism was founded by a small group of people led by brothers Charles and John Wesley. Through popular momentum it grew apart from the Church of England in the 18th century and developed as a forward-looking, evangelical doctrine that espoused not only spiritual worship but also good works in God's name. Methodists petitioned for justice, reform and social welfare and worked among the poor, widows, orphans and prisoners. The religion continues with popular support to this day.

In the early 19th century a group of Methodists in the potteries area of Staffordshire led by a gentleman called Hugh Bourne, feeling that the faith had somewhat lost its way from its original purposes, attempted to re-establish some of the basic evangelical tennets

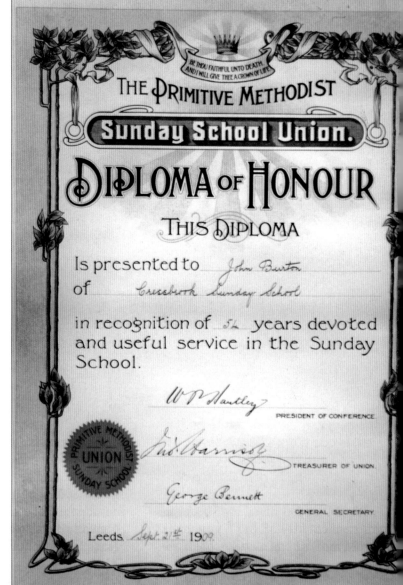

Diploma of Honour awarded by the Primitive Methodist Society to John Burton in recognition of '54 years of devoted and useful service'

of Methodism and reduced the form of worship to one centred on the worshipper rather than the place of worship. In 1807 Bourne organised and led an open-air worship at Mow Cop, which may not seem out of place in a modern religious society but it caused something of a stir among the leaders of Methodism at the time, who labeled the action *'Highly improper and likely to cause considerable mischief.'* The event was highly successful, however, and was attended by about 4000 people. A further event organised by Bourne resulted in him and his followers having their membership of the Methodist Society withdrawn. Undeterred they set about establishing their new, simpler form of worship under the name of *Primitive Methodism*. Primitive Methodism proved to be a highly successful and popular mode of worship. Being centred on the worshipper meant that it was portable and could be taken to all places and all people. Primitive Methodists could worship wherever Primitive Methodists were and even the smallest and least appointed hamlets could temporarily co-opt a room in a house for a place of worship. The faith found fertile ground in the Peak District and in Cressbrook, which as at this time the village did not have a church or any other formal place of worship, it thrived.

It was introduced in 1844 by John Oldfield, who came to the village from Tideswell. Mr Oldfield and the Primitive Methodists of Cressbrook

Turf cutting ceremony for Cressbrook Chapel. Mrs Mallison holds the brolly over Mrs Waterhouse of Lomberdale Hall while Mr Mallison looks on

used his house as a place of worship. A trend that continued for many years as the leadership of the local society passed between individuals. Over time the society was led by William Jackson, William Hayward, John Burton and his daughter Hannah after him until, in 1931 the Trinity Chapel was built and consecrated on the land immediately opposite the Toll House for dedicated use as a place of worship by the Primitive Methodists of Cressbrook. Within living memory 23 Lower Wood Cottages is still referred to as the *Chapel House*, reflecting its recent use as a place of worship before the building of the Trinity Chapel.

The notes that accompany the order of service for the opening ceremony for the new chapel imply that up until this time the patrons of the estate of Cressbrook, namely the McConnels and the Worthingtons after them, were not supportive of the Primitive Methodist society. The notes state that

'Recently land restrictions, hitherto preventing steps toward the erection of a church, have been removed. The estate, compact and picturesque, among some of the most beautiful Derbyshire scenery, is now in the hands of those favourably inclined'

There was, however, no restriction on the building of churches, just on the building of churches specific to this faith. This is demonstrated by the fact that in 1902, some 30 years earlier, Mary Worthington had built the Anglican Church of St John the Evangelist on land at the top of the village, adjoining the Sunday School house. The Worthingtons, while not overtly obstructive of the evangelical Methodists, clearly preferred the formality and reflective worship of the Anglican faith.

The estate of Cressbrook passed from the Worthingtons to Dickie and Mallison in 1925 and their now benevolent and supportive patronage is revealed in further passages of notes, where it says of the turf-cutting ceremony for the new chapel, performed in the previous April ...

'... Alderman W C Mallison presided ...'

while the celebratory thanksgiving service that was held at the school in the evening of the day of the turfcutting was …

presided over by M Dickie, Esq, Ravens Tor'.

The order of ceremony notes also state that Alderman Mallison complemented the Cressbrook Society on raising sufficient funds over the last five years to start the project. Clearly the purchase of the estate in 1925 by Dickie and Mallison marked also the arrival of a regime that made the acquisition of land from the estate for the construction of a dedicated place of worship possible, where it had not been previously. In the five years between Dickie and Mallison's purchase of the estate and the turf cutting ceremony on April 19th 1930, the community raised the sum of £800 toward the project, while eventual costs reached £2000. The fortunes of the Primitive Methodist society of Cressbrook however, followed the fortunes of the mill and after its closure in 1965, with few people left to worship there, the chapel was deconsecrated and passed into private ownership as a house.

The church of St John the Evangelist passed into the control of the Anglican church when the estate was broken up. At present the vicar, Frank Yates, administers to four churches locally with Cressbrook having services on the second and fourth Sunday in the month.

A railroad through the valley

A railway link from Derby to Manchester through the Peak District was first proposed in 1840, approved in 1846, built in the 1860s and eventually closed in 1968

The section of the line from Ambergate junction in the south to Rowsley opened in 1849 but the precise route northward beyond this was a matter of debate for some time despite there being only two real choices; either the Derwent Valley through Chatsworth Park or the Wye Valley through Bakewell. The latter was agreed upon when the Duke of Rutland, across whose land the railway would have to go, lobbied the House of Lords successfully in favour of Bakewell which had much to gain from its connection to the rail network. Even so, construction of the line from

Rowsley to Buxton did not commence until 1860.

The construction of the railway and the inevitable despoilment of Monsal Dale infuriated many, including the notable philosopher John Ruskin, who commented on the development in his monthly pamphlet, *Fors Clavigera* where he railed at the developers. Some of this text is inscribed on the information board on the Monsal Viaduct so is well known to visitors walking along the Monsal Trail. The original plans for this section of the railway did not include a stop in Monsal Dale but on being approached

JOHN RUSKINS OBJECTION

'You think it a great triumph to make the sun draw brown landscapes for you. That was also a discovery, and some day may be needful. But the sun had drawn landscapes before for you, not in brown but in green and blue and all imaginable colours, here in England. Not one of you ever looked at them, not one of you cares for the loss of them when you have shut the sun out with smoke so that he can draw nothing more, except brown blots through a hole in a box. There was a rocky valley between Buxton and Bakewell, once upon a time as divine as the vale of Tempe; you might have seen Gods there morning and evening - Apollo and all the sweet muses of light - walking in fair procession on the lawns of it, and to and fro among the pinnacles of its crags. You cared neither for Gods nor crags, but for cash (which you did not know the way to get): you thought you could get it by what The Times calls 'Railroad Enterprise'. You enterprised a railroad through the valley - you blasted its rocks away, heaped thousands of tons of shale into its lovely stream. The valley is gone and the Gods with it, and now every fool in Buxton can be in Bakewell in half an hour and every fool in Bakewell in Buxton, which you think a lucrative process of exchange - you fools everywhere.'

Monsal Dale station in 1910

by the McConnel's in 1863, the Rowsley and Buxton Construction Committee agreed to put in an additional stop at Upperdale where it could be accessed easily from the Mills. A simple siding, called Cressbrook siding, was incorporated into the build for the unloading of coal for the mill and there was also a livestock dock for transporting cattle from local farms. At this time the road from the junction at Upperdale to the station was improved and the river crossing, until this point no more than stepping stones and a ford, was supplemented with a footbridge. Although never economically used by the local population, the station was nonetheless popular for many years with country walkers, especially on summer weekends. Freight traffic was restricted almost entirely to coal for the mill which prior to its conversion from water to steam turbine in the early 1900's amounted to not much more than 400 tons a year. With the conversion to steam turbine this rose immediately to around 1500 tons per year and peaked in the 1920s at around 9000 tons per year. The system had been run by the London Midland and Scottish Railway until British Rail took over and the railway through Wyedale ceased to all but occasional and holiday traffic in 1959. By this time the mill had converted to mains

The footbridge at Upperdale

THE VIADUCT, MONSAL DALE, DERBYSHIRE. 255.

electricity and no longer took coal from the railways and apart from a very infrequent bus service, this very rural community has had to rely on its own means of transport since the closure of the railway in 1968.

In 2003 the Derby to Manchester Rail Project, a partnership of organisations led by Derbyshire County Council, was launched to assess the viability of re-opening the line. A series of mobile exhibitions visited 10 places close to the proposed route giving out further information and questionnaires to visitors for feedback and analysis of public opinion on the proposition. A public meeting was held at Cressbrook Club in July 2003 which gave people a chance to put questions to those closely associated with the proposal. The 'Question Time' panel

The Monsal Viaduct is 70ft above the river with semicircular arches, each having a 50ft span

included Tom Levitt Labour MP for High Peak, Lord Edward Manners from the Haddon Estate and Dr Tom Moat

The Monsal Trail - which uses the disused railway track - is popular with walkers all-year-round.

from English Nature. The meeting was very well attended on a rainy evening with many people standing outside on the steps of the club, unable to get in. One of the crucial factors to the re-opening of the line was how this would affect the Monsal Trail, a feature of the Cressbrook landscape and popular with walkers in the Peak National Park. The line would also pass through, or close to, several SSSIs (Site of Special Scientific Interest) and other

Monsal Dale station c.1910 showing both platforms and tracks

conservation areas recognised as being of European importance.
This controversial project was eventually shelved as the consultants determined that there was not a strong enough economic case for re-building a rail link. Also, the environmental case that there would be a potential benefit from using rail over car was not proved.

between **the lines**

ISSUE TWO

Time to have your say

MANCHESTER STOCKPORT HAZEL GROVE CHINLEY CHAPEL CENTRAL MILLERS DALE MONSAL DALE/ GREAT LONGSTONE BAKEWELL ROWSLEY DARLEY DALE MATLOCK MATLOCK BATH CROMFORD WHATSTANDWELL AMBERGATE BELPER

Local stations omitted for clarity

BUXTON

ON TRACK

Ken Munns was railway signalman who worked for many years in the signalbox at Monsal Dale. He recalls here details of the railway operation on this rural link

Ken, with two young visitors in Monsal Dale signal box

"

KEN MUNNS

I joined the railway about 1943 down at Derby and came down to Monsal Dale as a signal man in 1961 and I was there until they closed it in 1966. I'd been in a job that I wasn't really suited to so - I went on the railway as a junior messenger and I was there till March '45 when I joined up and went into the Fleet Air Arm - same as Arthur - and when I got demobbed I went back on the railway again. The company then was called London, Midland and Scottish Railways until nationalisation and then became British Rail. First I went to a signal box at Millers Dale for about three weeks and then came down to Monsal Dale. Millers Dale was a very big station with five platforms and the post office used the station facilities. If you wanted something from there you went to the window where you bought a ticket. Derek said when he first started on the post office he was actually at Millers Dale and used to go to the Wriggly Tin Café and when I was at Lime sidings Bert Spratt, a signalman at station box lived there. It's closed now.

So in a signal box, you got roughly nine weeks training, for rules and regulations more than anything. There was three of us in the box and we worked three shifts and you worked with the same feller all the time when you were learning but as I say I was only there about three weeks and then I had to come down to Monsal Dale for about 18 months - something like that. After that I got another job at Bakewell and I did what they called a porter guard job at Bakewell Station. I used to work the seven thirty five out of Bakewell down to Derby, come back on the cushions -

Ken in Fleet Air Arm uniform

yes, on the soft seats like a passenger - and then work my day out on the platform. I was there just over 12 month I think and the job was then given back to goods guards at Rowsley, so I got reverted back to Great Longstone station. I was living at Longstone probably, I can't remember the exact date 1951 something like that and I went working for a building firm. But I came back again, that was in '56 and the day I started at the Lime sidings the old chap at Great Longstone station had heart attack and died, old Sammy Wright, so they shoved me back to Longstone again because I knew the job. I was at Longstone about nine months, something like that and then I got back in the signal box at Monsal and came back to living at Cressbrook. I met Vera, well I started going out with Vera, about '57, '58. The signal box was smaller at Monsal Dale, only a 12 lever frame where the one at Lime sidings was a 24.

Bakewell box I think that was about a 20 lever frame, something like that I'm not sure. You could work the Monsal Dale one on your own on eight hours a shift and we averaged about 45 trains a shift or something like that. They run all night - you see it was mostly freight trains. There was a lot of freight and there was a passenger service of course. The stopping trains used to be a 4.18am from St Pancras, which was a parcel train and went through to Manchester and in between that you'd the Buxton parcels at 6.45am from Derby which was at Millers Dale at 8.15. Then there was the Nottingham

" *Duffield, Belper, Whatstandwell, Cromford, Matlock Bath*

Liverpool which left Nottingham at nine o'clock and that was the one I used to travel back 'on the cushions' when I was on the guards job. Stopping passenger trains at Monsal Dale well there was four on the up line and five on the down line. The 8.20, 11.15, 2.15 and 5.15 that was on the down going towards Millers Dale and then coming the other way, there used to be the nine o'clock, twenty to one, the next one was tea time twenty to five then another one at six o'clock. It was same service at weekends apart from during the summer time, they ran a late one that stopped at 8.28 down and 8.54 up - Saturdays only. And they'd run a hikers' train on a Sunday, probably two trains, one in the morning and then they came back at night time - hikers used to come off in droves. Day return was one and threepence I think from Bakewell and Buxton was about one and nine pence day return, something like that.

In those days you were issued with a uniform and you had to wear it even in the signal box. Sleeve jacket, sleeve waistcoat - yes, they were optional whether you had one with sleeves in or one without. Well invariably you ordered sleeveless one time and another time you'd order one with

sleeves in cos they're handy in wintertime.

It was warm in the signal box as we had a little stove to cook bacon and eggs on it every morning. It was only a little square stove with an oven above the fire and we used to toast the bread on oven bottom and go out in the field and get mushrooms.

It was under Dr Beeching who said he were closing the line and that was it

full stop. The line didn't actually close until '67 but they took the signal box to pieces and they just burnt it same as they did the station - one of the plate layers had some of the windows out of it for a greenhouse and the signals were just left in an off position. The trains were still running up to some

left: Monsal Viaduct - now part of the Monsal Trail
above: Ken working the levers
below: Ken wearing his old BR uniform at Monsal Dale station

time in '67 but it used to close at weekends anyway, used to close on a Saturday night till Monday morning. We used to have a switch in the box that you turned and it cut the box out once you'd pulled the signals off, just switched it through the two boxes either side.

I was offered a job somewhere down Nottingham way so I said 'Oh that's no good to me,' I wanted to stop round here. So I went back building again

and in '67 '68 I think the line closed all together. "

End of term report

Cressbrook Schools' role in the life of the wider local community is recorded in its official log. Extracts give a view of school life during the early and mid 20th century

Cressbrook School was founded by the McConnel family in 1878, leased in 1906 by Derbyshire County Council who eventually purchased it in 1936. At first it was a private school for the mill workers' children who attended for half the day and worked the rest of the day in the mill. When the school was taken over by the County Council the leaving age was 14 and following the 1944 Education Act, children left at 11 to attend Tideswell Secondary Modern or grammar schools in Buxton or Bakewell. Cressbrook Primary school was attended only by village children until pupils from Litton Mill enrolled when their school was closed in 1948.
A weekly log was written up by the headmaster and gradually over the

years the information in the logs was more informative of life-style and events happening outside school life.

Attendance figures fluctuated greatly throughout the early 1900's, mainly caused by bad weather and illness, usually colds and whooping cough but also mumps and measles which swept through the school population as there was no immunisation programme in place. The logs in the early 1900's were signed by James McConnel as chairman of the school managers with appropriate comments: *"Pupils do not attend as they should and have been warned. Sometimes through illness, weather or with no explanations at all. Accommodation for pupils hats and cloaks is needed."*

In March 1906, Matthew Dickie from Cressbrook Mill, as one of the school managers was the signatory for the logs when there were 90 pupils - 54 juniors and 36 infants whose ages ranged from three to seven years old. H M Inspectors visited once a year and gave reports which were also entered in the school log. In September that year it was noted that in the mixed age class there were 68 children which the Headmaster had to *"manage and teach alone for $^1/_2$ the week when the pupil teacher is not available. Desirable for help to be provided."*
In the infants there was *"no syllabus and no evidence to show lessons had been prepared."* The condition of the premises was noted and *"will receive attention in due course."*

The following March of 1907 there were still 90 children on the school register with eight children under five years old and six part-time workers. The annual HM Inspectors report noted that there was still no help provided for the headmaster as had been suggested the previous year and in the infants department *"owing to the congested state of the room it was difficult to give the infants a suitable school life. Desirable that the youngest children should not be admitted."* There was still no accommodation for hats and cloaks and the infants cloaks were just piled in a heap *"a most unsanitary arrangement."*

At a school managers meeting in December 1908, the clerk was instructed to write to the school

inspectors to inform them that *"no children under three years of age were to be admitted to the school without the sanction of the school managers."*

After the inspectors visit of **1909** there was a better report. The school was now suitably staffed to cope with 80 children on the roll, the buildings had been improved and were more *"tasteful and cheerful although some pictures would be a valuable improvement."* the infants section still needed improving and *"it was regretted that children of three were still being admitted."*

By **1913** the number of children on the roll started decreasing. Only 53 were on the register and never reached the overwhelming number of 90 again. Occasionally there was no teacher for the infants so the top girls in the juniors would work with them. Remember the school leaving age was 14 and some of the girls - not the boys - would go on to be pupil-teachers.

A new teacher in **1915** complained about the lack of exercise books and that *"the attainment of pupils is below average and will need much more effort from pupils and teachers to bring it up to standard."*
During the period of the first World War between 1914-18 there were a few references in the school records to the war. On Empire Day in May 1917 it was recorded that in the morning the children talked about the Empire,

Mr T.H.Savage, head master at the school was a keen cricket player and also played billiards at the Institute. But his greatest pleasure was playing cornet in Cressbrook Band and occasionally used to appear at the school with his cornet tied with red, white and blue ribbons

below left: School line-up early 1900s

patriotism and food rationing. There was no television, radio or highly visual newspaper coverage to report up to the minute events from abroad unlike today with instant reporting and comment. School closed at noon on Armistice Day the 11th and all day the 12th of November 1918. A holiday was given by the managers to celebrate peace.

Even though in the early **1920**'s a doctor, nurse and dentist made regular school visits for health checks the log sadly reports in October 1920 the death of Charles Beresford aged five of diptheria and by the end of the year there were more reports of children absent with the illness but with no further deaths.

An immunisation programme for the prevention of diptheria was not implemented until 1941. Mumps, measles, chicken pox and whooping cough went round the school like wildfire as again there were no vacination programmes as there are today. At one point the school closed early for Christmas because of an outbreak of measles and on reopening in January there were still pupils absent through illness.

By **1922** more social aspects of school life started to be recorded when the school was divided into four houses. Green House with S.Bingham as captain, White, H. Bingham, Blue, W.Smith and Red, B. Lloyd. Unfortunately there are no further

mention of the benefits of this, other than a report from the nurse who noted the children *"were particularly clean and tidy owing to a system of marks awarded for tidiness"* and there was an improvement in general cleanliness, again with marks awarded.
There were big Empire Day celebrations in May as an acknowledgement of King, country and the outside world. There were special lessons for the 40 children on how to march, salute and to learn the words of Empire songs. On the day itself, May 24th, parents and friends were invited to the school for the programmes of events starting with the hymn *The Old Hundredth*, followed by *Land of our Birth* and *The Red, White and Blue*. Then there was a march

past, saluting the flag, the crowning of the May Queen and dances by the older girls. A playlet - *The Making of the Empire* - had every child taking part in the Tableau finale and singing of the *National Anthem*.

Scrumping for apples - that well-known pursuit of young kids - even happened in quiet, rural Cressbrook. Mr Swindell, chief engineer at Cressbrook Mill who lived at Old School House next door to the school, made a complaint to the Headmaster that schoolchildren had rifled his apple trees while he and his family were on holiday. The culprits were discovered and were made to apologise and bring *"a penny towards damage done."* All did except for three boys and a girl - they *"forgot their pennies."* Mr Swindell accepted their apologies but none of the money.

HAPPY DAYS?

" **ISOBEL SUTCLIFFE** When I went to Cressbrook School, I went in the little room first with Miss Alsop, she was the teacher, and then when you were older you went in the bigger room with Miss Fawcett. Miss Alsop was nice, she was a very nice kind lady, but Miss Fawcett had got a very bad temper, she had red hair, it was red as fire. I enjoyed school, but I was always thinking about her because you know, you were frightened, when you went to bed at night you were thinking about the next day, what would it be like, you were always wondering if she'd come or if you'd get the day off.

VERA MUNNS We were well educated, but the hard way... we had a ginger-haired teacher and she didn't mind giving you a clout or two for anything, anything. It wouldn't be allowed now. She hit my brother one day and I told my mother and she went in the afternoon... she clouted me and said go and tell your mother ... So I got a double dose in one day for no good reason. That was when her temper was up and yet she was so good-hearted when she was alright.

MARGERY HOYLE The head teacher was Miss Fawcett who had red hair and a temper to match. We used to learn just the three Rs and the occasional sewing lesson. She was a very strict teacher, not many people liked her, because of her temper really. I mean she was probably a good teacher, but you had to get your letters right. When you started with your joined up writing it had to be absolutely perfect, your loops on your G's hadn't to be blotted, you know if you had blots you had to do everything again. It was just not on and you got a slap or cane or whatever. Oh yes, she wouldn't get away with it today. "

With a smaller number of children than in the 1900s and an increase in teaching staff more could be achieved as in 1925, when the school inspectors report commented that the children read well, especially poems read by younger children but *"older children as is so often the case in remote villages, are somewhat shy."* Shy just isn't a word that can be applied to today's Cressbrook children!

With nearly fifty children on the roll, a new teacher was recommended to the position of headmistress in October 1927. A person who still stirs up strong memories - even today - of her teaching methods in those who were taught by her. Miss Lillian Fawcett, with the red hair and temper to go with it lived at Windmill and cycled into school every day whatever the weather.

Girls in school having been taught hem-stitching *"have taken much pains with the work"* used their needlework skills making tea-towels, tea-cosy covers, egg cosies and scarves and money made through sales of this work went towards purchasing a new carpet for the platform in the main school room. Having started in spring 1930, £2-5-00 had been made by October 1931 towards the total cost of £2-19-6p and the new carpet arrived at the end of the year. It was the first record of pupils' collecting money through their own efforts.

In 1930 two free places and a scholarship were won by children for further education and Miss Fawcett received a letter of congratulations from the school managers *"to place on record their appreciation of your efforts to improve the general standard during the past 12 months."*

In May 1932 Vera Swindell entered the Elocution Contest at Buxton Festival and came 2nd in an entry of 18 winning a certificate and medal. The debate on hunting doesn't appear to be new as the first school debate was recorded in the school log *"Is hunting cruel?"* There was no report on the result. From July to December that year there were many children off sick with either chicken pox, whooping cough or mumps and Blackpool seems to have been a popular venue for parents to take their children for recuperation.

Spring 1933 and there were only 38 pupils but enough of them to receive a football in return for the 120 Oxo wrappers which they'd collected and sent in. I hope the boys occasionally let the girls have the football as their two playgrounds were still divided by a wall and this didn't change until

School line-up around 1930

was decided that Tideswell Co-operative society *"will supply pupils with milk on each schoolday."* Regular visits from school inspectors noted that there was a much more structured educational timetable and the children were *"keen on the plays The Tempest, A Midsummer's Night's Dream and Twelfth Night."*

At the managers meeting in January **1937** it was proposed and unanimously agreed that Mr Swindell be appointed Chairman of the school managers in place of Mr Matthew Dickie who passed away on 13 August 1936. And after ten years at Cressbrook School, Miss Fawcett resigned to take up the Headship of a larger school in Somerset. Miss Verna Goodwin took over from Miss Fawcett as headmistress.

The number of pupils decreased from 1936 and by the end of **1938** there were only 13 children attending the school and Tideswell Co-op didn't consider it worthwhile bringing so few bottles of milk every day so discontinued the service.
A visit by a Physical Training Organiser suggested that the wall dividing the two playgrounds should be removed as this would be a great improvement for the boys and girls playtime activities.

School line-up - 1938

1938 when the wall was removed.
In May 1933 Vera and Isobel Swindell again entered the Buxton Festival Elocution contest. Isobel came 3rd and Vera 5th and both were invited to recite their pieces the following week at the Tideswell concert for local Musical Festival competitors.
The standard of reading and writing was high in the school and the current book being read was *Lorna Doone*. Library books were delivered to the school on a regular basis. Even the pupil-teacher Margaret Green aged 14 attended fortnightly French classes in Bakewell and with the title Rural Pupil Teacher awarded, the following August she received her first small salary for August and September.

At the Buxton Festival in May **1934** Isobel Swindell won a cup and silver medal and Hazel Lupton and Margery Furniss gained 2nd and 3rd places for recitation.
The County Medical Officer visited the school in October to find out whether the 31 pupils were *"desirous of purchasing milk"* - not free yet! This was followed up by a demonstrator from the National Milk Publicity Council for Derbyshire who gave a lecture on the subject *Milk and its value*. As country children with a farm in the middle of the village who had fresh milk delivered daily straight from the churn to houses in Cressbrook, no lecture on the value of milk was surely needed. However from the beginning of December it

Pat Kelly, with cousin Jimmy who were evacuated to Cressbrook from Chorlton Park School in Manchester pay a visit to their old school

A telephone had been installed which made complaining about the faulty boiler more effective as the low temperature in the school often made it impossible to work. Even with the installation of a new boiler there were problems as coke which had been ordered arrived late and the temperature in the school fell to 44 degrees. Together, illness and bad weather over Christmas and New Year meant that only six children arrived for the start of the new term of 1939.

September **1939** and school re-opened after the summer holidays under uncertain circumstances owing to *"the international situation"* and the school was closed for two weeks because of the evacuation of children. On re-opening there were three evacuated children admitted, together with two more children from Sheffield, all on a separate register

with a teacher from Chorlton Park School in Manchester assigned to them, making a total of 12 children altogether. As the weather was exceptionally cold in September the caretaker was asked to put the heating on which he refused to do - the temperature was 45 degrees. Perhaps he was thinking of the colder Peak District weather to come in the winter or the possibility of coke deliveries being delayed, or even rationing. A test was made to discover how long it would take the children to reach home from school in the event of an air-raid. Miss Verna Goodwin, the new headmistress, informed the committee that she proposed to get married. Throughout a large part of the schools history the school managers committee stipulated that single female teachers had to resign their position when they got married and the committee agreed to her temporary retention for the

duration of the war, or until otherwise determined.

In **1940** the schools started to be involved in war efforts - quite different from WW1 where there were few mentions at all of events abroad. Metal foil and metal caps were collected for the Red Cross and it was decided to collect books and magazines for the troops. Coke supplies for the boiler were still haphazard - so the caretaker was right - with the school having to close for two weeks in February until it was delivered. The school was also rewired and the electricity was now supplied by the Notts and Derby Electrical Co. Empire Day was celebrated in May with a collection being made *"to provide cigarettes for the forces."* Air-raid practice was carried out by the 20 children now on the roll and scholarship tests were taken during this period, but they were awarded to three evacuees. By September there were now two official evacuees, four private evacuees and 11 village children. The school was sometimes used for dances and there were always complaints from the caretaker about the state of the premises after these events had taken place. One of the complaints was about the parquet floor which had been left in a dangerous state having been highly polished for a dance held there. Cleaning sand had to be put down to prevent the children from slipping over. As well as sorting out the boiler and problems caused by

enthusiastic dances held on the premises, the caretaker was instructed to apply anti-splinter net to the windows as soon as possible. The school was let out to the staff of Columbia Pictures Corporation who had been evacuated from London and taken over Cressbrook Hall, for recreation during their time at the Hall. They were charged 7s 6d each time the school was used and there were regulations of course. The rooms had to be *"swept, furniture replaced, no intoxicating liquor to be taken onto the premises and all breakages paid for."* The school was also let out to the Soldiers Comfort Fund committee at a charge of 4s 0d a time.

Empire day in May **1941** was again used for a collection for cigarettes to be sent to the forces and letters of thanks from the troops for cigarettes supplied arrived in the autumn. From the Autumn onwards the school began to close early because of the blackout and it also started later in the morning. One of the English periods was used to check gas masks and to learn gas drill. The children in the school had regular health inspections and 14 children were taken to Tideswell for immunisation against diptheria. A special effort was made in the National Savings Certificates May campaign for the *War Weapons Week* collection in the Bakewell area and a total of £157-10s was invested.

January **1942** and the Air Raid

> **GORDON AND MIRIAM SHARPLEY**
>
> **Gordon:** I was born in this village in 1941, 10th January 1941 and I was five when I went to school, down to the school at the bottom and my parents used to take me down. The first day I went it was Mrs Bennett, the teacher, and when I first started I didn't want to go to school and I stood near the radiator in the cloakroom and as soon as she turned her back I was halfway up the hill coming back home. Peter Worsencroft caught me and took me back to school. Peter was a character called Wuss, they always called him Wuss didn't they, he didn't want to be known by Peter, it was always Wuss and he was one of the older boys when I started. It was him that fetched me back and took me back to school. He was at the school yes, he was older than me and lived in the village, next to the school.
>
> I don't remember the ginger-haired teacher at all but I mean they did tap you, I mean they'd tap you on the back of your hand or just a little clip round the ear hole or anything if you misbehaved, which you expected in them days but you daren't come home and tell your parents that you'd been naughty because you got another one.
>
> **Miriam:** I was born on 1st of the 1st 1939 in Litton Mill. I started at Litton Mill School and then the school closed in Litton Mill, about 1948. I was seven when I came to Cressbrook School that had got a canteen, because at Litton we used to have to go down to the mill in Litton Mill for our lunch and children came here from Litton Mill ever since till Cressbrook closed. We didn't walk along the bottom, we had transport from Litton Mill. It's quite a long journey all the way round from Litton Mill and there was no short cuts. I was at school with Gordon and we did a play once down at school and I always remember we were only about seven or eight and we were Mr and Mrs Gamp in this play together.
>
> **Gordon:** When Miriam was down at Cressbrook School I fancied Miriam but she said she doesn't remember me.
>
> **Miriam:** September 1962 we got married in Tideswell Church and we lived in Cressbrook ever since. Well I have, Gordon's lived all his life, I've lived here 42 years.

Welfare made plans for the school to be used by the village as a Rest Centre. During *Warships Week* in March collections totalling £61-10s were made to invest in National Savings Certificates. In spring, lilies-of-the-valley were gathered from the dale to sell and raise funds towards buying instruments for a school percussion band.

A schools inspector arrived in June to make enquiries about providing hot meals for the children. Mr Dickie at Cressbrook Mill was consulted but thought it *"unlikely that a canteen would be established at the mill"* and it was decided that Litton Mill canteen was impractical to supply food because of the difficult access on the roads, especially in winter. Columbia Pictures were also approached and *"it is probable that arrangements could be made to feed the children in their canteen."* As there were only nine children at the school at this time this wouldn't have been too much of a problem, but unfortunately the possibility that Columbia Pictures would be leaving the Hall was confirmed by the company, so other arrangements had to be made.

A representative from the newly formed Milk Marketing Board also called to discuss the proposed *Milk in schools* scheme which was hoped would start in September. A total of five local farmers were approached to supply milk for the school and each producer stated his inability to do so. Mr Swindell attached a lock to the gate of the school yard because boys had been roller-skating in the yard out of school hours.

In February **1943** a large consignment of Air Raid Welfare goods arrived and was put into safe storage in the school with only authorised people allowed access. In May £71-11-11d was invested in school saving certicates for the *Wings for Victory* drive.

By January **1945** it was still proving impossible to make a firm arrangement for school milk to be supplied. It was suggested that full cream dried milk should be supplied to the children for a trial period. Again there was a problem as there was no means of preparing this in the school. This was solved by the caretaker at the time Mrs Swindell, who lived next door at School House, who undertook the preparation in her house. When all the supplies had arrived the school milk scheme finally started in May. In March the Rest Centre stock was removed - the only shortages being one steel helmet and one tin of beans. The school was closed on May 8th and 9th being declared a National Holiday for the celebration of *"cessation of hostilities against Germany."* In June the education department in Derby suggested that by supplying a cooker, the necessary equipment and advertising for a cook in the local papers, meals for the children could be produced on school premises. The job would be for up to four hours a day and include a free meal with a salary of £52 per annum. There were 16 children on the register in September.

From 2nd September **1946** school milk was FREE. The register showed 20 children attending the school although it was recorded that there was only enough seating for 18 children. In October there was the first mention in the school records of the possibility of the school being closed down and strong objections were recorded by the Board of School Managers.

January **1947** was recorded as having very bad weather with low school attendance and at the beginning of March a blizzard cut Cressbrook off and the school was closed from the 4th until the 8th of March. Records also show that Litton Mill School was also closed from the beginning of February until the middle of April because of the severe weather and the lack of fuel for heating.
Plans for a school canteen started taking shape in 1947. The piano in the small room would have to be moved to make way for a kitchen area to be installed and as the piano was the property of the village, everyone having subscribed towards its purchase, it was decided to move it up the hill to Cressbrook Institute.

In **1948** Mrs Furniss was appointed as

the cook for the school canteen which opened on March 16th with 21 children staying for dinner. A cheque for £6-5-0d for 300 school meals consumed over two weeks in November was sent to the Divisional Education Office and school milk was now being supplied by Chatsworth Express Dairy.
An urgent meeting was called by the managers of Cressbrook School after receiving a letter from Derby Director of Education. It was suggested that owing to the failure of the committee to employ a replacement teacher at Litton Mill School following the resignation of Mrs Harrison, arrangements should be made to transfer the children to Cressbrook School as a temporary measure. It was hoped that further efforts would be made to obtain a teacher so that the school could re-open. The managers pointed out that the road between the schools was dangerous for the young children to travel unsupervised, the alternative route by bus or other transport being approximately six miles. They suggested that as a bus already left Litton Mill with the older children attending Tideswell Purselove School, the younger ones could go with them and be taken on to Cressbrook School. Litton Mill School was officially closed on July 19 1948. The Divisional Office needed a suitable person to make a daily check on the building for maintenance and Mrs B. Bingham was recommended at a salary of 7s 6d per week from August 1st 1948.

During **1955/56** 19 pupils were on record as attending the school.

In September **1960** plans were submitted for a complete refit of the canteen area with new formica tops, cupboards, sinks and draining boards.

In November **1963** it was reported in the school managers logs that the Divisional Education Executive *"have taken note of the fact that the number of children actually residing in Cressbrook could be reduced to nine if those residing at Litton Mill were transferred to Litton."* The school committee couldn't overlook the high cost of maintaining a local school for nine children when there was another school in the area which could accomodate the Cressbrook children.

In **1965** when Mrs Daykin started as headmistress there were 16 children, in 1966 18 children and in 1967 there were 21 children.

September 18th **1968** Mr W. Swindell resigned as Chairman of the school managers. He'd served on the managers committee for 41 years and been its chairman for 31 years.

It was noted in the school managers reports in **1976** that there were now only 26 children attending the school, owing to the fact that many of the houses in the village were holiday homes and there was no way of altering the catchment area.

School line-up - 1987

> *"when they closed the school just a certain light went out of the village"*

CAROL HARLAND

There was about five or six of us all went down to London in 1987 and we all put different articles together to give them our outlook on village life and the school and the environment where we live and why the school should be kept open. We were successful, so we invited them up here because the Minister was interested in the band as I'd put forward that we'd got the brass band and it was very successful at that time. I said if you're interested bring your instrument, if you're happy to come and have a blow with them, they'd enjoy it, anyone who can do it come and have a go. He didn't come but we'd actually saved the school. It lasted for a few years before closure started coming up again and we started raising money once more. I gave my services free of charge to open up the school and get it all ready for doing teas and that and I used to do it once a month with another parent and we used to serve all the walkers and people who came with their cars or whatever. Could have anything from soup or anything you wanted, we used to make and sell the food and then give all the profit to the school. We did do quite a few thousands of pounds-worth in total. Some we spent on the school and the rest was still in the bank account when the school finally closed and we split up the money between the children as they went in their different directions. It was a shame, but looking back on it, it wasn't a bad thing in the end. The children went to schools which we wanted them to go to and they've done well so we can't complain.

Save Cressbrook School

DEREK COOKE

When the school closed I thought it was a great loss, great loss. When you got down to about twelve pupils the only way it kept open so long, there was so many children coming from outside the village into the school that kept it going. I think that was one of the things that had a big effect on the slowing down of the village. I can't say the death of the village when they closed the school, just a certain light went out of the village especially down at the bottom. It was just a part of village life that wasn't here any more. You know they always reckon the main thing in the village was the pub, which you've never had apart from the club, the shop which after the Co-op closed there wasn't one and then when the school closed and the children went out of it a part of village life went with it as well.

left: Happy days at Cressbrook School

The last school picture at Cressbrook School in 1997

TAKING THE REGISTER

Mrs Daykin started as headmistress at Cressbrook School in 1965 expecting it to shortly close. She was still there 25 years later

" MRS DAYKIN

I was teaching at Taddington School having been widowed and having a young daughter. When the area director visited the school he asked if I would consider going to Cressbrook School because the numbers were low and they were considering closing it and wanted somebody to keep it going in the meantime. I agreed to attend an interview one evening at a governors' meeting, well they called them managers in those days, and I duly went along with him and was appointed as Head of the school. I asked if they would mind if I brought my little daughter with me, and one of the fellows said 'No that'll be fine, bring your little girl along'. So I started after the Whitsuntide holiday in 1965. They'd had a number of temporary people and it wasn't very satisfactory having people for short periods and I was expecting the school to close nearly all the time I was here, so it wasn't a very settled sort of

situation. The threat of closing quietened down and nothing was said about it and if I mentioned it to the director he'd say 'Oh well you can forget it for the time being' and that sort of thing, so I just kept carrying on, I was so happy here. I was the only teacher here and the numbers started increasing and of course I had them all from beginners - four years to eleven and it wasn't easy by any means so I asked for some help of some kind. Mrs Gratton came as secretary then Mrs Lindley came, part-time teaching so many mornings a week to take the infants. When she left Mrs Rhodes came and she was here for the rest of the time with me. I think I'd been here ten

years when she came, but she was only part-time of course taking the infants and I had them in the afternoon. They did increase her time a little for a while and then they'd cut some down and then they'd give it us back again. So it went on like that all the time. The number of children

fluctuated a lot. When I first came I'm sure there were only seven - I brought my little girl she made seven and then they built up you see until we were about 30 with 18 children from three families.

Major events like the Buxton Choir Festival we entered every year. We had all the juniors in the choir and one or two out of the infants section. There was a category for small schools you see so we came in that and we used to win. Cressbrook is a different type of school altogether, but I don't suppose we thought about it at the time you know, we all carried on achieving excellent results. We took part in everything necessary along with other

Mrs Daykin takes the children on a mini train trip in the Pavilion Gardens, Buxton

> **I remember women used to come walking in at lunchtimes straight through here to the telephone, they were coming putting bets on at this 'phone**

schools. Parents became more involved as other times of day you never got the fathers interested at all. You never saw the fathers and then the time came they were just as interested, we had both parents together coming to parent evenings and out of school activities and our concerts were extremely popular involving three generations. When I taught at Taddington I don't remember any of the fathers there at all, so it was definitely a change.

I arrived each day at about 8.40am and prepared for assembly which we had each morning. Then if time allowed I would do some administrative work. Mrs Furniss and later her daughter Merlyn Bingham was in the kitchen - she didn't come till 9 o'clock but the caretaker had opened the school. We would ring the bell, then take the register. We sang at assembly, said a prayer, there was a story or something like that and the children all stood round but on Friday mornings we had ¹/₂ hour hymn singing when chairs were brought round the piano. Then

would follow maths until playtime at 10.30. At 10.45 we settled down again for various English subjects whilst the afternoons would be devoted to either geography, history, science, art, music whichever was on the timetable for the day. We had some form of sport each day after play in the afternoon, and we had an annual sports day. The infants

had their own timetable when Mrs Rhodes was there. She and I were often still in school at 5pm. There was only one period when we hadn't got a cook in the school kitchen and that was the only time the school meals were brought in. I tried to get the room as a classroom when Mrs Furniss left because we were so cramped in here you know, with infants here and juniors up there. It wasn't easy at all, it was difficult when I had them all together from age four up to 11, but it was even more difficult when I had an extra teacher here teaching the infants because we

were in the same room. But the county wouldn't allow the change, they said it must stay as a kitchen. I've forgotten what reason it was for now but it wasn't allowed anyway, so we stayed as we were until I retired and meals were brought in from another school until a new cook was employed and meals could be cooked here again. The mill was still operating when I got here because I remember women used to come walking in at lunchtimes straight through here to the telephone. I stopped them and asked what's all this about and they said 'Well we've always done it,' and I said 'Done what?' They were coming putting bets on at this telephone, so Mrs Furniss said 'I've told them you wouldn't let them do it.' About three or four women would come in and they'd all such long faces when I stopped them - I didn't hear anything about any winnings. The train was still running and taking the railway line up didn't affect us at all, I can't really remember them doing it, but I do remember us going for walks along the track for nature walks.

We went and met the Queen when she came to Ripley in 1977 when she was there at the Police Headquarters and granted Derby the honour of becoming a city. We wrote two songs and gave

Decorating the walls of Cressbrook School with their own art-work

them to the Queen as she walked by. Jackie Sharpley, being the oldest pupil, presented them to her. We used to have lots of trips out and when we went to London we had a special train for us. We joined the train at Chesterfield and it said Cressbrook School all across the carriage. Another time we went by coach when we visited the Tower of London and also sat in the House of Commons, joined by our MP of the time. We did all kinds of things, the trouble is we couldn't do it for everybody every year so some children would miss out on certain outings but there were other different events each year. Then in came this stipulation that primary schools were not supposed to go further than a certain distance, so we were

handicapped in that respect. The children only wore school uniform when we did the concerts and when we went for a day out they all wore the uniform. We stopped wearing it when I had an upset with one of the parents. One of the boys, I can't remember who he was now, but he turned the heating off, fiddled with a tap in the porch and we were flooded. It was cold and we couldn't have any heating on so next day a girl came in trousers and one of the children came and told me so I had a little word with her. "You know, we don't allow girls to wear trousers in school." The next day one of the parents rang to

complain, "It's these trousers, there's nothing in your booklet to say girls shouldn't wear trousers." Others complained that the uniform wasn't warm enough, so we only used it from then on for outings and special days. Also, the authorities at the time were

> **they said the staff weren't sufficiently trained to cope with all the different subjects, but of course in a school like this you had to teach everything**

of the opinion that the uniforms denoted an elite. Bullying was frowned upon, punishment was they'd miss their playtime or some other pleasurable occupation. Sometimes they wrote lines usually a piece of knowledge for them to remember. Closing the school loomed up when I was about at retiring age and the County Council made out it was for various reasons, but it was really economic. They maintained that we hadn't got enough staff to cover everything. We'd done satisfactorily up to that time and the parents rebelled against it and called a meeting, fought for it and it stayed open. At that time they were closing small schools because they said the staff weren't sufficiently trained to cope with all the different subjects, but of course in a school like this you had to teach everything.

Performing in a school pantomime production of 'Cinderella' in 1975
The picture includes John Bunting, Lesley Holmes, Paul Archer, Jeremy Hall, *kneeling:* Jackie Sharpley, Margaret Waterhouse, Louis Harland

A busy craft lesson with Mrs Daykin

CAROL HARLAND

Merlyn Bingham's mum, Mrs Furniss, used to be the caretaker, the cook, the bottle washer and everything. I went to Mrs Daykin and I said the caretaker job was being advertised. She said 'Well, its been put up for advertising but we've got someone doing it because as you know Mrs Furniss isn't 100% so Hazel's been doing it.' Then Hazel moved to Tideswell and got re-married so the job did come up for grabs so Mrs Daykin said I could apply, which I did and I did that for about 24 years.

Caretaking involved cleaning of the school, doing the boiler which was a coke boiler when I first took it over. I used to have to shovel tonnes of coke into the boiler room 'cos the fellow couldn't get it in and he used to leave it in the back driveway down to Dale Terrace. So we had to move it all and generally I looked after it. Outside loos had to be whitewashed and what have you and generally look after the school. Then it got that we got an oil boiler so it was a lot easier and the toilets were also built inside so it got that we was quite modern.

1989 - the annual school photograph with headmistress Mrs Daykin *left*

The Cressbrook School Christmas concert was always a popular village occasion and always played to a packed house

"OUR EVACUEE"

Pat Kelly was evacuated to Cressbrook in 1941 and writes vividly of her stay, which was longer than that of other children who were sent from Manchester

Pat Kelly amongst the evacuees from Chorlton Park School Manchester making their way to the station

PAT KELLY
I arrived in Cressbrook "The day war broke out!", eight years old with my identity card, a small case full of clothes, gas mask and rations with I think, six other children from Manchester but I was the only one who stayed. I didn't know what evacuated meant. I thought it may be inoculated or exterminated and I didn't want to leave my home and go to a strange place for whatever it was. In the carrier bag should have been butter, cheese, milk powder, egg powder, three tins of condensed milk and three tins of corned beef but we'd been bored on the train and swopped what we didn't like and I loved condensed milk so ended up with a carrier full of condensed milk. We waited outside the Methodist Chapel until it was decided who was to go where. Eventually another girl called Jill and I were taken down to Lower Wood, the first end stone cottage where were introduced to the lady who I grew to love and who looked after me like a grandmother for three years - Mrs Lomas. She was horrified to discover that I only had condensed milk in my rations as the nearest shop was in Tideswell.

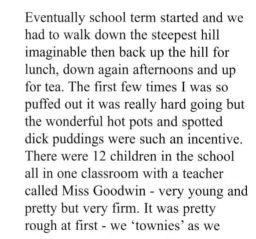

> If the sky was red and the bombing sounds were on the right it was Sheffield and on the left it was Manchester

Eventually school term started and we had to walk down the steepest hill imaginable then back up the hill for lunch, down again afternoons and up for tea. The first few times I was so puffed out it was really hard going but the wonderful hot pots and spotted dick puddings were such an incentive. There were 12 children in the school all in one classroom with a teacher called Miss Goodwin - very young and pretty but very firm. It was pretty rough at first - we 'townies' as we were called were constantly set upon by the village kids but my new pals took my side and I had a better time than the other evacuees in the village. The expected air raids did not materialise here nor the gas warfare and eventually the other evacuees went home one by one until I was the only one left in the village.

Some nights from my bedroom window I could see the sky bright red from the fires caused by the incendiary bombs and we could hear the german planes flying over at night and got to know which were the 'Jerries' and which were ours by the engine sounds. If the sky was red and the bombing sounds were on the right it was Sheffield and on the left it was Manchester and I used to say my prayers.

After a time I was no longer a thin delicate child. The fresh air and exercise I was getting plus the huge meals I was eating after five miles a day up and down that hill paid off! When my father came to see me during one of his leaves from the Air Force he was amazed and I remember him saying I had footballers legs and he was so happy to see me so very fit and strong. I even won the occasional fight with the village boys who came to respect this 'townie' a little more. Mrs Lomas was very religious - Methodist chapel. I went to church every Sunday and Sunday School in the afternoon. We had a different minister every week, Mrs Lomas's son was a minister and they always came back to our cottage for tea. I was introduced by all the villagers to everyone who came as 'Our evacuee'.

Pat Kelly with her cousin Jimmy, outside Lower Lodge, Cressbrook Hall

I think they were quite proud to still have one as most of the others, even in Tideswell and Litton had returned home in spite of the raids.

When Mum and Pop came to see me they brought Aunt Doris and Uncle Harry with cousins Jimmy and Peter. Jimmy loved Cressbrook and they arranged for Mrs Lomas' sister-in-law to have him in the next door but one cottage. It was nice having my cousin there and although he put up with a lot of aggro from the village kids at first, like me he was eventually accepted. Eventually Doris and Harry rented one of the lodges belonging to Cressbrook Hall as they wanted all the children safe as the air raids were getting more frequent and heavy. Tay - our older cousin - came to live there, looking

after Jimmy, Peter and Paul and Mum and Doris came often to get away from the raids. I was always happy to see them.

There was no 11 plus in those days but you could take what was called a 'scholarship' but it was optional and most of the village children went to the secondary school in Tideswell and left at 14 to get a job. So it was a very proud moment for Mrs Brett - she was Miss Goodwin and had got married - when cousin Jimmy passed his scholarship and went to Lady Manners. The next term I was asked if I wanted to take the scholarship and I said 'no' because my friend Peggy Walker wasn't taking hers. Mrs Brett wrote to my parents and they insisted I was to

never neglect opportunity

S. R. Brett.
1. 10. 41.

sit for it. At the time I had an autograph book and asked her to write something in it. She wrote *"Never neglect opportunity'*. I sat my exams completely alone in a large classroom and Mrs Brett kept arriving with more papers, it seemed never ending. I returned to Manchester and I went to Ardwicke Municiple School which I hated. I was caned by the headmaster for standing on a bench to look out of the window, it was awful. One day I came home to hugs and kisses. I had passed the scholarship for Whitworth Senior High School at little Cressbrook School!

"

Happy family gatherings at Lower Lodge Cressbrook

A FARMERS WIFE

Harriet Allen farmed Home Farm with her husband Matt for nineteen years. A time of milking by hand, saving chickens from foxes and storms while bringing up six children without todays mod cons

" **HARRIET ALLEN**
I first went to Cressbrook May 1939 where my husband was a farmer and we got the chance of working the farm at Home Farm. My youngest son was three months old when we went there and we rented it from Stanton Estate who owned the farm. It was a very uncomfortable farm because we were down in the valley, it was very nice to live there but it wasn't for my husband because all the land was at the top of the village. It was a dairy farm and my husband delivered the milk to all the houses in Cressbrook and he had a white horse called Star pulling a float. My husband used to take milk down to the mill but it was for the manager and I think his secretary. The mill workers, the biggest part of them lived in Cressbrook and that's where my husband used to go, to every door

and anybody that wasn't in always left a jug at side of the door with a saucer on top. On her cart Star had old fashioned silver milk churns with the lids that you push on the top with milk ladles for a quart measure, pint and a third of a pint. Today you'd not be able to do it but in those days there weren't many cars and she used to move from one point to the next and at Top Row she used to wait for him at the bottom of the steps where the War Memorial is. Of course later on we had a tractor but my husband found out that it was so expensive to run a tractor because going up hill with loads of manure, coming back again with loads of hay it was taking the tread off the tyres and within two or three years he had to have new ones. We were there 19 years, so my husband said 'We'll just have to move we are subsidising the farm.'
We had 20 to 30 cows,

short horns and Ayrshires and we had to milk them twice a day - that was hand milking - we got a building eventually up there - Robinson's woodyard it used to be - and in the summer time we milked them up there. But in the winter time they never went out, they stayed down at the farm in the buildings because there were some suitable buildings here. We kept a few female calves in the herd if the parent was a good milker and to begin with we did have a young bull and it came from Chatsworth. Then he got very bad-tempered so Matt got rid of him and that was when Queenie, our other horse, went at the same time. After that we had the AI which was a good idea. It was a lot safer because when you turned this bull out you never knew if he would you know, get out into the village so we decided and especially

Harriet Allen

when he got bad tempered, to get rid of him. He wasn't to begin with but they do as they get older, some of them. When we came to Cressbrook in 1939, the mill was working in those days you know, we enjoyed it, we liked it and

" *she used to move from one point to the next and at Top Row she used to wait for him at the bottom of the steps where the War Memorial is* "

when the war broke out we became a close community. It was handy for the children for school, they didn't have far to go which suited me and Ken, my youngest, used to sneak off if he got a chance when the others were playing out in the playground to join them. We did have a shop at the top of the village, it was the Co-op and Hancocks from Tideswell they used to come. I've still pots and pans from the day I bought from Alan Hancock when he used to come round. That's all he sold was pots, pans you know all sorts of stuff like that and paraffin. Another part of Hancocks family they were grocers that lived at Tideswell and they used to come and take orders for

> ## " and what didn't go in the river, the fox had been and chopped their heads off "

groceries, so it was handy. And there was Big Frank and his friend - can't remember his name - but he drove the small open-sided lorry that delivered vegetables and fruit and they lived in a house on the way to Longstone Moor. If I wanted to do any shopping for clothes or shoes I had to go by bus to Bakewell and to get there I first used to have to walk to Monsal Head. To begin with they used to bring the mill workers by bus at half past seven in the morning and then they used to come again at 1 o'clock. If you went

left: Matt Allen with 'Queenie'
below: Maureen and Brian Allen sitting on 'Star'

with them you had to go right round by Tideswell and by the time you got to Bakewell it was time to come back so I caught the quicker bus from Monsal Head and had about an hour in Bakewell. I'd push the pram up the hill with two little boys in it and then leave it in the yard of the people who used to live in the two cottages up there, until I came back. Then it was back again down that hill and I walked that many many a time but Maureen said "Well it must have done you a lot of good Mum all that walking" 'cos I'm 87, 88 this July.

Columbia Pictures came during the war for two or three years, I don't know whether they were there any longer but they were there two or three years - yes, definitely three years. They were the administrative side of Columbia Pictures and it was the boss that came and he brought his workers with him because the lady that stayed with me was his secretary. Some stayed at Cressbrook Hall and others were billeted in the village amongst us people. I used to get them regular for

glasses of milk, that's what they used to come for and of course if it was a wet day they'd generally land in the house and sit down and have a chat. We sold the pigs on, apart from when the war came and we got rid of the pigs except for one to fatten. We'd a couple of neighbours out of Pancake Row, they each had a pig a piece and we always did it so that we'd got the pigs ready at different times so we didn't clash. Then we helped and we

Mary Swindell with Matt and William Allen admiring the pigs

shared with one another. The pigs were slaughtered on the farm by someone we knew, Mr Bacon from Great Longstone. He used to come and kill the pig with a humane killer and then they were hung up in an outbuilding and the blood was drained into one of my big pancheons, if you know what I mean by pancheons. I think you will do, big bowls, earthenware bowls, they're brown on the outside and creamy colour on the inside. One of the ladies, Mrs Broomhead that lived

left: Maureen and William Allen in front of the ivy-covered outside toilet

right: A trip out with neighbours Mrs Worsencroft and son Peter, for William Allen

Harriet with young David and Ken Allen in the driveway of Home Farm

in the Row, she always used to make the black puddings and I wish you could get black puddings off her today 'cos they were proper black puddings not in the skin, she did them in basins. Well I know milk was one thing that went in and bread crumbs and a few, what they used to call groats. I don't know what groats are - I think that it's barley. A few chunks of fat but she never put much of that in, oh and onions, she used to put onion in. Then you boil it, you steam it, a bit like a Christmas pudding. I used to do it in my copper for them and my husband had made a kind of a platform so they wouldn't touch the bottom cause you had to put a cloth on the top, greaseproof and then a cloth and tie it

before taking the biggest part of an hour to cook. Afterwards it would keep properly and besides in those days people had a good cool pantry and stuff would keep for ages. My pantry was very cool because it never saw much sun, especially in the winter. You shouldn't kill a pig in the summer, you only kill it when there's an R in the month really, so that's when it used to get done. We never sold the meat no, it was given to the people and the hams we used to salt and then you bagged them later and just hung them up till you're ready for them. It wasn't salty like it is today, it wasn't honestly, and they used to make brawn, that was with the pig's head. You used to take the stuff out of the pig's head and then add bits of pork, you know when they were trimming the sides and it made nice brawn, it spoils you, you know, when you've had home made stuff and you buy the shop stuff now.

We had biggest part of about 100 chickens. Yes, oh yes, we sold those

eggs and what we didn't sell, Thornhills from Great Longstone collected. We also sold them at the door - we'd no trouble selling them. We had a very bad storm once at Cressbrook many years ago, I can't just remember when but it was a wild night and we had a field near the mill with a hencote and we'd got 50 point of lay pullets in there and then came this terrible wind and it smashed the hencote up and took it right down the river and it landed up at the water fall. Yes, at the Horseshoe Falls so we'd no pullets left. That was it yes, and what didn't go in the river the fox had been and chopped their heads off. There was a chap that lived in Pancake Row, what's his name... Worsencroft. Fred Worsencroft that's right and he used to have a gun 'cos of the foxes taking the hens and that's the first time I'd ever seen a fox close up. He used to shoot them because I know Isobel had one off him and had a fox fur made. Mr Broomhead also had hens and he reared rabbits for shows and

they were kept down in the place called The Shivers, in a shed full of hutches and a hencote as well, so the foxes knew where all the chickens were. Our chickens were just laying chickens and then when they'd done about three or four years we used to sell them in the batch and then get some more. We sent away for them as we hadn't time to rear our own, because you need an incubator to put your eggs in and we used to send away to a very good firm I know in Scotland and get a delivery of hen pullets arrive on the train, the train was running in those days. We used to get baby chicks and we had to rear them but it wasn't like starting from scratch, or bothering with hens. We did try just at first to begin with but then my husband said 'Oh I'll have them in a batch and then we can, you know, just have them in the cote and concentrate on them like that.'

We had special lanterns which gave off heat and the storm lanterns were just for light because we didn't have electricity in the building. You had to be very careful not to knock it over or it'd set the place on fire. Once, when Matt was filling the tractor with TVO one night, a splash fell on the storm lantern. It just exploded and the fumes set the tractor shed on fire and the wooden floor above, where there were hens. One of the older boys ran to Isobel's to phone for the Fire Brigade from Bakewell but by the time they arrived the fire was out as we'd soaked a lot of bags and mats to beat the fire out.

We also had a flock of about 20 sheep which we kept on Longstone Moor as well as keeping the few pigs and poultry. The sheep had to come back in winter and be housed, but they were up there in the summer. The sheep we used for lambing, having lambs to sell on so when we brought

> ## *" it spoils you you know, when you've had home made stuff and you buy the shop stuff now "*

them back from Longstone Moor it was well timed in winter to have them indoors for lambing. My husband used to have them lambing late, so as they could go out soon as possible which was the best idea generally into that field at the bottom just past the mill. Then they got moved up on to Longstone Moor. We walked them up there, 50 sheep and their lambs with our working dog, a very good black and white collie called Lassie. She spent the nights in an empty pigcote and worked during the day. Lassie came from Fearns at Wardlow, they used to keep a lot of sheep and had collie dogs and we used to join them with the washing, you've heard of sheep washing? We used to go to Ashford-in-the-Water to get the sheep washed, used

far left: Norman Allen, Matts brother
left: Harriet with Lassie

to walk them there and back from Cressbrook. Well, you decided amongst yourselves a time or day to take the sheep down to Ashford and we very often joined Fearns and of course you would have to know which were your sheep. But they were marked yes, they were marked and they've got an instinct who they belonged to anyway. Well, they washed them first and then later on they're dipped with disinfectant and one of these chaps, I know his name was Fearn, he gave my eldest son our collie puppy and she, oh she was in her teens when she died. I know we had a few ducks and when she wasn't working with Matt or anything she'd spend her time getting these ducks back into hencote and she just got them right up to the pop-hole in the cote and pushed them right in as if to say, well you go to bed now even if it were day time.

Our other horse Star, she used to do the quibbling jobs as Matt called them such as sowing in the potatoes. Yes, sowing in the potatoes, that's when you take a plough, or what ever it is and you can walk down between the rows. We had turnips and cabbage and of course it gets rid of the weed when you do that and Star used to do that job.

That was up at the top - its nice south facing up there. Harvesting the potatoes was always done when it was the holiday time for the children and we used to get lots of school children come, that was in October 'cos they have a holiday then. Paid with potatoes, that's how they were paid. Some of the women used to come and help to pick potatoes with the children and Matt used to collect the potatoes in the bags and bring them down home to that loft. He used to cover up the floor with them you know, to just dry them, then rebag them and then any that were damaged or anything like that he outed them and then people got a proper bag of potatoes, not with some squashy ones in. Matt would gather the turnips up and bring them into a pit and then cover them up and then just use them as he wanted them. They were for the cows and to eat yes, but cabbage he left growing in the ground and just fetched them when we wanted them, but they were all grown at the top of the village. Yes, there's always a job to do. We did get a tractor but we still kept Star and we kept Star right up to she died. We had her put down eventually because she got to that stage, she was in her thirties and she'd get down and then she couldn't get up again. My husband used to always make sure to get her up but he said to me I think I'll have to put her down. We were very upset about that but he said people might report him and say we was causing a lot of suffering. *"*

77

The interior of the mill after the final closure

The end of an era?

The mill closure was the end of an era as redundant tenants moved away in search of other employment and houses were sold on by the mills creditors to incomers

For years the fabric of Cressbrook: it's houses roads and services had been assets of the mill- a private estate with very little in the way of externally owned property. This fact, together with the villagers' dependence for their livelihoods on the mill might suggest that its closure would tear the heart out of the village and leave it to decline. Decline inevitably came but it was less pronounced than might have been expected.

The school had been leased to Derbyshire County Council in 1906 when Dickie and Mallison extended their initial lease and the roads through the village had been transferred into the care of Bakewell Rural Council in 1909. Consequent to the mill's failure in 1938 the remainder of the assets were transferred to Robert Bingham and The Stanton Estate Company whereupon the school was immediately sold on to Derbyshire County Council. Much of the remainder of the assets stayed with the creditors until the mill finally stopped operating for good in 1965.

Although now detached from the mill, the village was still owned by large, independent third-parties who chose to rent out the properties. The village thus continued as a private estate in all but name. While there were families who had been in the community for decades, the population was still essentially tenancy-based and itinerant and had changed over the years as workers came and went. Henry McConnel in particular had regularly rotated his workers around the various mills owned and operated by his

Cressbrook Mill from the pond

company. Also, while for the most part the houses were rented to the people who worked at the mill, there were some in the village that were rented to people who worked elsewhere locally. Certainly after 1938 Robert Bingham and Stanton Estates had no vested interest in accommodating only mill workers in the houses, so a growing percentage of the population of the village was not employed by or dependent on the mill. As tenants, the people of the village were free of the millstone of a mortgage, which under economic catastrophe could have dragged many into poverty and the village into ruin. When the mill finally went bust therefore, there was actually very little to hold the redundant workers to Cressbrook and with a minimal amount of inertia the population was free to move away in search of other work; while those people living in the village and already working elsewhere were essentially unaffected economically by

events. A more direct impact was felt by the gradual closure of the facilities such as shops and the post office caused by the significant reduction in monies coming into the village. So while the community as a body of people living in a common space suffered an initial collapse, individual suffering within that community was less pronounced. It is no doubt true however, that the death of the mill, the end of the way of life followed by its employees and the long, significant line of history that it represented was

The mill around 1900

Robert Bingham died in August 1977, after which his estate and fortune was entrusted in perpetuity for the benefit of the local community.

With the mill now gone and unable to pay its creditors, it was up to The Bingham Trust and The Stanton Estate Company to realise some return on the investment they had made in previous years in acquiring the mill's debts. So it was that gradually the houses in the village came on to the open market. As tenancies were surrendered, the houses were sold off into private ownership. Not that either creditor was particularly pushy in this process and both were prepared to wait for the houses to be freed up by natural order while the rents asked from the remaining sitting tenants have been modest.

Unlike in the boom's of the 1980s and 1990s the houses were not snapped up nor did they demand the shocking prices that property in the village can now fetch. In the mid-1970s the housing market was very much against the village. The attributes that today make Cressbrook such a desirable place to live; tranquillity, remoteness, lack of services and facilities, acted against it at a time when brand new housing in purpose-built estates was affordable and desirable. The houses, well over 100 years old by this time, still had many of the original services and features with which they had been built, including outside toilets and no central heating. Many of them were

very small by modern standards and despite the attention to detail when they were newly built could now be classed as little more than hovels. Some were even condemned. Anyone taking on a house in Cressbrook was thus faced with the extra costs of bringing it up to date. This hampered the easy liquidation by The Stanton Estate Company and The Bingham Trust of bricks and mortar. Most of the houses sold into private ownership around this time fetched under £2000 (equivalent in 2002 to at most £25,000 according to Economic History Services) and required a similar amount to modernise. The first house transferred from Robert Bingham into private ownership was 41 Middle Row, which was sold in 1974. Old School House was sold by the Stanton Estate to Mostyn and Sheila Davis in 1970 but it took 12 months to gain planning permission to improve the house and be able to move in. When they bought the property it had no windows in the triangular shaped kitchen, one cold tap and an outside bucket toilet which was emptied weekly. Stanton Estates split the cost of putting in two septic tanks with Mostyn and Sheila so that all the cottages on Pancake Row could have inside toilets and bathrooms. Since then buyers for the houses in Cressbrook have been a mixture of sitting tenants, new professional incomers and investors. Some people have chosen to live in Cressbrook as their only place of abode. Some have bought the houses as quiet retreats in addition to

sad. It is a small blessing that the population never had to face the crushing economic realities suffered by the workers at the end of coalworking in north Nottinghamshire or the end of shipbuilding in the north-east of England which left those communities utterly destitute.

Despite Cressbrook Mills demise there were still other mills operating in the area and many of the skilled workforce readily found employment. Dormer

Mill in Chinley in particular, took many workers from Cressbrook and the daily twilight bus picked people up first thing in the morning and delivered them home in the evening for some time until those workers had moved closer to their new place of employ. Inevitably, the tenancy for the houses changed hands to be replaced by people working more locally. So began a new phase for the village as a place from which to commute.

The mill in a state of disrepair

their first homes and some have bought them as investments for either long-term or holiday home lets. While Cressbrook is an indisputably beautiful and profitable place in which to own property, holiday lets inevitably make it harder for the village to function as a community, or to hold the attention of local government as a deserving beneficiary of the services enjoyed by larger communities.

The Peak District National Park is an area of outstanding natural beauty and attracts millions of visitors every year. This popularity is a direct result of its proximity to the large conurbations of Manchester, Bradford, Leeds, Sheffield, Nottingham, Derby and Stoke-on-Trent, which are within easy drive of its moors and dales. It also brings in people from much further afield, both nationally and internationally and many of the villages are popular and regular

holiday destinations. Cressbrook itself is not a tourist honey pot and is even completely missing from some road maps, but it still sees a significant number of visitors passing through in the form of walkers, cyclists and motorists. Curiously, although it is very close to one of the Peak Park attractions, Monsal Head, which on beautiful days attracts hundreds of visitors to appreciate its spectacular vistas, Cressbrook remains comparatively quiet. Those who do venture away from Monsal Head, along the valley to Cressbrook either along the Monsal Trail or along the valley floor, rarely get further into the village than the mill. Many divert at this point into the beautiful Water-cum-Jolly Dale or up into the Cressbrook Dale National Nature Reserve. With few attractions beyond its history, there is little to bring the visitors into the village. The Peak Park exerts a preserving influence on the places within it. All development is very carefully controlled and must be in keeping with

local character. Cressbrook has not escaped this and has changed very little from the state in which Mary Worthington left it in 1904 while additional restrictions apply through the location of the village within a Conservation Area. The net effect is a feeling of old-world charm about the place. The drivers for this preservation are understood by the villagers but there is at the same time a frustration, certainly from the people who lived here before both the Peak Park and the Conservation Area existed, and a feeling that they are being denied the social progression available to communities not similarly restricted. There is also a relative dearth of commercial opportunities in the village, coupled with strong limits on the ability to develop them exerted by the Peak Park. The village cannot therefore exploit its position as a

potentially strong attractor for tourism. Those who live in Cressbrook must therefore be content with its tranquillity and beauty as these are its most viable and perhaps only assets.

The 1985 Housing Act vested in local authorities the power to serve compulsory purchase orders on listed buildings that were deemed to have not been adequately or suitably maintained. Although the mill itself had been listed in 1967 not long after it closed, in 1985 the houses of the village of Cressbrook were not listed. The Department of the Environment, later to become English Heritage, consequently listed the Victorian dwellings of Middle Row and Upper Wood, which even after 140 years were still more or less in the state that they were built. Lower Wood avoided listing because of the changes made to it during the course of its life prior to 1985. The owners of the

houses of Middle Row and Upper Wood thus suddenly had greatness thrust upon them with Grade II listing status and it was not necessarily welcome as living in a listed building places restrictions upon what can and cannot be done to the building, as well as the manner and materials in which changes are made. Thankfully the emergency powers available in the 1985 Housing Act have never had to be invoked in Cressbrook.

For those people who live in the village and who need jobs to pay for the mortgage, the village is largely a place from which to commute to work and car ownership is essential. Local public transport is limited to two buses per day in each direction and these are not timed to make commuting practical. By way of contrast, when the mill was in its later years and the motor car was becoming more popular, Cressbrook rarely sported more than one or two because it was a self-sufficient community. Even the metropolises of Tideswell and Bakewell were only a bicycle ride away. The disappearance of all of the village facilities consequent to the failure of the mill mandates ownership of a car to make the business of living in Cressbrook feasible.

The village is regarded very fondly by many of the people who grew up in it but almost without exception these people are denied the opportunity to live here because there is no such thing in the village as affordable housing or starter homes. Once the

Cressbrook Mill - an illustration
by Keith Hislop

houses in Cressbrook had moved from their relatively poorly serviced and undesirable state into their present attractive and highly desirable state their increase in market value was inevitable. The recent housing price boom of the 1990s in particular has seen the market value of the houses soar way beyond anything that could be afforded by the incomes of most working people, let alone those who grew up here. The net effect of this has been to artificially jog the demographics of the village to exclude people that would normally be buying their first homes. When houses do come onto the market most young people simply cannot afford them and this has reduced significantly the number of young families in the village. This has resulted directly in the closure of the school, which lacked enough pupils to justify its continued existence. Those few children who remain in the village are obliged to go to schools in neighbouring villages and while the fact that schooling is available in Great Longstone, Litton, Tideswell and Bakewell is laudable, it only further discourages young families from settling in Cressbrook. The turnover of house ownership in the village is relatively low, with properties rarely coming onto the market. This has resulted in a relatively stable population in recent years in spite of the economic upheaval. The major social and economic drivers that shape any community are the availability of local work, the availability of local housing, the availability of local schooling and location. These in turn drive the price of local housing. None of these drivers are set to change in Cressbrook in the foreseeable future. It is reasonable to assume, therefore, that the pattern of living in the village has been set for some time to come.

AUBREY HOWE

Since the mill has closed there's been a vast change there's no two ways about it, and you can't compare like for like because to be honest with you life's changed. It's gone forward or whatever you want to say, people live different lives now. The car has made the difference to Cressbrook. I remember two or three buses, North Western buses, picking the work people up. And you know that was the only way they could get to work, nobody had cars or, very, very few cars you know. It has altered a lot and the thing was everybody tended to work at the mill then, all the children went there, the grandchildren went there and the houses was rented off the estate. All that's gone and it'll never be there again, it has definitely altered. I could have bought Pancake Row for £1000, from one end to the other but my father said leave them alone, all you'll end up with is just the slates and the stone because there was no water toilets or anything, and they'll condemn them. The old people living in them were paying about five and six a week, expecting a ton of work done on them. But its no good looking back over your shoulder. Stanton Estates really wanted to get rid of them, and sold the houses down the Wick at Ravensdale at about £150 a piece. Stanton Estates really in a way gave Cressbrook away.

And don't forget when my father bought Leisure Farm there was no electric and no water there. My father actually paid to have the electric put in and it cost a lot of money. We had such horrendous winters in those days it used to bring the lines down, so my father applied to have the electric cable. He had to pay over five years and I think in those days it was £40 a quarter which was a terrible lot of money, going back 50 years. He did it and you could burn whatever electric you wanted in that quarter, but you had to stand £40 whether you burnt it or not. And the water came in 1952, Wades bought that, it came from Bamford Dams. I remember them blasting down through you know, and it comes along on the top to Cressbrook. We got water toilets virtually as soon as we got the water and could put septic tanks in. Cressbrook has altered a lot since the mill went and it'll never be there again, so it has definitely altered, there's no two ways about that.

The restored mill in 2005

CAROL HARLAND

The mill closing made a difference. I think if you talk to the very old they'll say 'Oh its nothing like it was' and I don't think they can accept that it's got to change, people are moving all the time. But its lost its identity of a mill community because the mill is all gone and its lost a certain amount of the closeness. The children aren't educated here on the doorstep, but they are learning different things and they're mixing with different cultures and different things all together. There's no one here what was brought up with me now, they've all moved on. People were wanting to move away because when Dick actually told his friends that he was coming to live at Cressbrook they thought he was mad. They said 'You're not going and living in that hole?' He said 'Why not, my wife's lived there all the time.' 'It's dead, you don't want to go and live there.' I think that was what happened, because everyone I went to school with went in different directions, none of them stayed. Not one. I think its happened again because I know my daughter Nicola would have loved to have lived here but she can't afford to, and Neil would have loved it, well, he's still at home but he can't afford to move out because he can't afford a house so he's living with us. Its gone in waves sort of thing, you know it's coming back but they just can't afford to live here now. I think one or two, they would have put their roots down in Cressbrook if they could afford it, but they can't.

Maureen Allen pays a visit to the empty school yard of Cressbrook School

CAT FLAPS & OTHER PLACES

*Part of Cressbrook life for over 20 years, **Derek Cooke** remembers the ups and downs of a village which was different to a normal posties round*

DEREK COOKE

It's about 24 years since I came here and my first impression of Cressbrook when I came around Stone Pit corner was one of wonderment. It was the view over the Dale towards Monsal Head and this quaint village clinging to the hillside I saw first and on down the village to the stunning view of the Hall and hills, then into Monsal Dale to Netherdale Farm before finishing my delivery in Ravensdale. It's a funny village really compared with others because there's such different parts of it. When you deliver it, you deliver it in blocks, you know the top row, the middle row and then down to the hall and then onwards after that... its quite a defined village compared with some. But another first impression was hills - everything was down the steps at the back of the house and it was all steps. I thought one of these days I'm going to break me neck down there you know and I never have done.

The theory is you gradually get to know the people. I know you're supposed to just pop the letters through and move on and so on, but it depends on the individual. You still get people who will just do the job and rush round but I like people and meet them and talk to them. Change a light bulb when it's gone or get coal in for some of the elderly people who were a bit, you know, couldn't do it for themselves sort of thing and at that time the postman was everybody's friend as you might say, they didn't look on you... well, I never got the impression that they looked on you with suspicion, people just accepted you because of the job.

I used to go into the school every morning about lunch time with the mail and the children would be having their dinner. They'd all be sat round, as you know the ages from about five or six right up to 11, I'd walk in and of course they'd all turn round - some sort of a distraction that they could think, 'Oh something's happened so we can talk instead of being told to be quiet.' The cook was Merlyn Bingham and when she went abroad, a young girl from Buxton took over for a while until it closed. I remember that 'cos her brother is a postman in Buxton. I used to have the odd ginger biscuit when they came out, some of the treats Merlyn used to make. When the school closed I thought it was a great loss, great loss. But there's been a lot of changes in the village as far as people's concerned since I first began the round, a lot of changes, people dying or leaving or whatever. There were a lot more people at home in the village at that time and as the old ones have died off, the young ones that have come in have to go out to work to support the house, so I don't see half as many people in a morning that I used to see. It's a very friendly place and just had a lull, about the early nineties when it just tended to die a little bit and now with a lot of the people that's come in you feel there's a resurgence in the village spirit again. This is where I think the new people coming into the village seemed to have cemented it together again. For

Derek on his rounds

Mr Cooke our postman

Mr Cooke is our postman we call him Mr postman. He comes every day at around 12:00. He helps us by bringing us our letters. Sometimes he brings letters for my... He is very friendly. Likes to chat to...

> ## " I thought one of these days I'm going to break me neck down there, you know I never have done "

instance you set off with one well-dressing and I think there's four now isn't there, one at the bottom, one in middle, and two now at the top? Yes, so this is what makes me think that you know the life in the village is getting back together, people getting back together more. I think one of the things the village missed out on was the school 'cos a lot of people

said they wanted a village hall in Cressbrook and the school would have made a great village hall but the opportunity was missed. Ann and myself were invited to the school when it did close, it was a great feeling to be asked you know, 'Oh I've been accepted' sort of thing. There's some interesting arrangements for deliveries - cat flaps, dog flaps, they are very, very handy at times. The dog flaps are just amazing they're so big - from a security point of view a disaster, but its amazing what you can deliver through a cat flap. But it does help if people have got a letter box. I know it sounds funny but nowadays you have people that still don't have letter boxes and that can be difficult for a postie. I've had sheds, coal bunkers, all sorts as long as people know where you've left it.

Comparing the villages I've delivered to, I should say its very similar, very similar, the villages themselves with there not being many people,

Derek cutting his post office van cake at his farewell party

people talk to one another, they're closer. You get into the big towns, they don't have the same contact and its just something that's just familiar with village life. There's a general air of trust in this village - I would say so yes, yes, I trust everybody, well over the years I just hope people... I think I know that they have, especially these last few weeks since I said I was retiring, some of the comments that have been made and I'm realising more now, you just assume that people trusted you and now I know they did.

After 40 years my body's telling me

that it's time to end work but same as Ann said when she finished work she didn't miss the job so much, she missed the people. 'Cos I've met some lovely people over the years and I've always been very, very happy on this round. Always had a nice feeling about the village, never any hostility which is what you get in some places. Yes, I've always had a nice feeling about the place and the people. I think that could be one of the things I'll miss most. I fell in love with Cressbrook on that first day, a feeling that **"** has lasted to this day.

ORAL HISTORY WORKSHOP

Colin Hyde from the East Midlands Oral History Unit, held a workshop on interviewing techniques at Cressbrook Club. He advised that chiming clocks, barking dogs and chirping budgies could disrupt a recording, but didn't mention cats being sick behind sofas, telephones ringing or coal being put on the fire. SYS, who transcribed the interview tapes, were impressed with not only the quality of the recorded tapes but also the content of the interviews.

Trinity House

Trinity House, a former Methodist Chapel is one of Cressbrook's newest buildings. **Jan and Gareth Watkins** *document one of the most chequered histories of any building in the village*

The story begins on April 12th 1926 when mill proprietors Matthew Dickie Junior Ltd sold a plot of land to 20 trustees of the 'Primitive Methodist' Church for the princely sum of £50. The plot, at the northern end of the village and just across the road from the Old Toll House, was situated on high ground with commanding views over Upperdale and Ravensdale. With the help of a £500 mortgage from the Primitive Methodist Chapel Aid Association - which was eventually paid off in 1941- work started on construction of the Chapel and was completed in 1931. The building was designed by architect Norman Palmer who worked for the architectural company JW Blackhurst of Sheffield. On July 25th of that year the opening of Cressbrook's latest place of worship was attended by the notable architect Edwin Lutyens (architect and designer of the Cenotaph in Whitehall, London) at a lavish public ceremony. Formalities commenced at 2.30 pm with the official opening and was followed by divine worship, afternoon tea (at one shilling per head) and rounded off with a public thanksgiving meeting. Music was provided by four guest vocalists supported by the organist from the Hope Wesleyan Church and, needless to say, the Cressbrook Silver Band.

The Chapel quickly established itself as an integral part of village life attracting an enthusiastic following. Many local residents were married at the Chapel, some of course had their funerals there; some both. Amongst the surviving documents from the Chapel's heyday are a new form of trust deed adopted in 1951 and an order of service from the 30th anniversary service in 1961.

By the early 1970s however the Chapel's best days were long gone.

Trinity House - a view not normally seen

Falling attendances meant that it became increasingly difficult to carry on. On November 21st 1972 the inevitable happened and the Chapel was sold by the trustees - including four of the original trustees who had purchased the land 46 years earlier - as a private residence.

Of course, certain restrictions were placed on the purchaser. The building could not be referred to as a Chapel any longer, hence the change of name to Trinity House and a restrictive covenant prevents the use of the

right: The original design of Trinity Methodist Chapel by architect Norman Palmer *far right:* The chapel before the fire in 1981

building for the manufacture or sale of intoxicating liquor, for the purpose of gambling, or as a public dance hall. The new owners of Trinity House were the Archer family who at that time ran a cycle hire company at Monsal Head. Carrying out much of the work themselves, the Archers completed the conversion and eventually set up home in the old Chapel. However on January 14th 1981 disaster struck when the house caught fire in the middle of the night. It was a disaster that could have been a tragedy but Mum, Dad and the two young children were fortunate to escape without injury - the family was safe but the building, alas was gutted. The Archers moved on, selling the derelict shell to another local family

with young children, Andrew and Linda Read, on June 7th 1982. Over the next few years the Reads devoted themselves to re-building and restoring Trinity House and shortly after completing the mammoth task in May 1988 the Reads sold up and moved. The new owners were the Watkins, 'incomers' into the area from South Wales. They continue the tradition of using Trinity House as a family home and a happy place to bring up young children.

Although no longer a public building, Trinity House continues to play an integral part in community life. Since 1990 in the run up to well-dressing week, claying and petalling of the village main well and the childrens' well has taken place in the garage.

The art of using a builders float to smooth out the clay before petalling begins, being demonstrated by Ken Munns, Ben Watkins and Paul Radcliffe in the garage of Trinity House to a young audience

DAVE AND ANN ARCHER
One Sunday in October 1972, having been walking in Derbyshire for the day we came back through Bakewell where we picked up the *Derbyshire Times*. Inside there was a reminder for an auction the following day October 8th at 3pm of three Methodist Chapels - Youlgreave, Tideswell and Cressbrook. By 3.15pm the next day Trinity Methodist Chapel was ours - for £6,500.

We had a son Paul who was nine years old, and he quickly integrated with the other village children - Julie Sharpley 10, Jackie 7, Stephen 5, Susan Oldfield 10, Mandy Gratton 9, Philip Bingham 13 and his sister Angela 11, Carol and Amanda Bingham and many more. For the first year we lived in a caravan at the side of the chapel and all the children treated it as their 'den' after school.

Early on the morning of January 14th 1981 the chapel caught fire. We were roused by the latest addition to our family, Sally, then aged three. She roused us early as she habitually did and we then heard crackling sounds from the fire and escaped with only a minute to spare, running downstairs through dense smoke, our son burning his feet on red-hot wooden

stairtreads. An hour later the main body of the building was burnt out with only its walls standing. The following day the charred remains inside were carpeted with four inches of snow.

Cressbrook Hall

Pig breeders, nuns, estate agents and an American film company have all been occupants of this nineteenth century mill owners' house in Cressbrook village

Henry McConnel had Cressbrook House built in 1835 as a family home overlooking Cressbrook Mill which he had recently aquired. The architect was Thomas Johnson, a notable architect of his time and the formal terraced gardens were designed by Edward Kemp, a landscape gardener who had trained at Chatsworth House under Joseph Paxton, famed for his design of Crystal Palace. In Edward Kemps book *How to Lay Out a Garden 1858* he describes Cressbrook House as follows,

"and the house is valued on being the only level piece of ground any-where in the neighbourhood. A pleasant stream winds along the valley at the base of the bank and a bare grassy hill rises abruptly from it on the other side."

As in most big country houses of this time there was a small hot-house and propagating house for the year-round supply of flowers and possibly fruit. The majority of the owners have mostly been sympathetic and respectful towards the Grade II listed building even though Cressbrook Hall has not always been occupied solely as a family residence. The change of name from House to Hall occurred in the 1940s and the various and diverse occupants have been a pig breeder, Columbia Pictures, who were evacuated there during WW2, an Irish order of nuns and an estate agent.

The present owners, the Hull-Baileys,

above: Cressbrook Hall, from *"a bare grassy hill on the other side".*
left: The Orangery at night

have spent the last 25 years repairing and restoring Cressbrook Hall to its former glory. The original Orangery has been restored as have the Victorian Gardens. This two acre site had variously been used as an intensive pig breeding unit and a garden centre. The walled garden area has now been turfed and the buildings converted into holiday accomodation.

In 1995, the Hull-Bailey family discoved Edward Kemp's original 1858 planting plan and embarked on

89

Owners/occupants/tenants of Cressbrook Hall

Year	Owner/occupant/tenant
1835	Henry McConnell - died 1871
1871	Isabella McConnell - second wife of Henry McConnell died 1885
1885	Mary Worthington - eldest daughter of Henry McConnell died 1904
1887	Unoccupied - or various tenants as below. Property owned by the Worthington family until 1933
1895	George Benton - Hackney breeder
1899	Alfred Herbert Dixon
1908	Reginald Stewart Milford
1925	William Mallison & Matthew Dickie t/a Matthew Dickie Junior Ltd
1933	tenants as above - owners
1935	The Stanton Estate Company
1939	Mr and Mrs J.R Ratcliffe
1941	Columbia Picture Corporation Ltd - tenants of Mr and Mrs Ratcliffe
1945	F.L.Attenborough
1948	The Presentation Convent, Buxton
1957	Edwin Hockenhull
1960	Ralph and Mrs Betty Johnson t/a Derbyshire Pig Hatcheries Ltd
1965	Derek and Mrs Mary Wilson
1979	L.Hull and Mrs B. Hull-Bailey

above: A concert given by Cressbrook Band in the newly refurbished Orangery
right: work in progress during rebuilding
below left: The gardens and Orangery
below right: Top Lodge, Cressbrook Hall

recreating his garden design. Many of the original species were re-introduced but it became apparent that the planting plan was probably a romantic Victorian idea since azaleas did not thrive in the strong sunlight on lime soil and the delicate fuschias were unhappy in the detached parterre on the east side of the property. At one time Cressbrook Hall employed 22 staff in the grounds and gardens and it may be that plants were moved inside or out as the seasons changed. There was no shortage of labour in Victorian England and the work of a gardner at the Hall was preferable to that of a mill worker.

The Chapel Anniversary Annual Walk, usually took place on the last Friday in May - the tradition probably originating from the Whit Walks which took place around the mills in Lancashire. This was an important date in Cressbrooks calendar when everyone wore their best clothes for the occasion, maybe even wearing a new hat. Over a couple of hours everyone would go in procession around the village accompanied by Cressbrook Band and at each stop there would be some bible readings by the preacher John Burton, Malcolm Burton's great-grandfather. Cressbrook Band would play some hymns, everyone would join in the hymn singing before moving onto the next place in the village. In this photograph, the bible is shown on a flower decorated trolley *(right)* The picture was taken in the early 1900s at Cressbrook Hall, probably by Malcolm Burtons grandfathers brother, who was a keen photographer.

Cressbrook Band

Dubbed variously over the years Brass, Silver or Public Band but now definately Cressbrook Band, local musicians continue to contribute to village harmony

Cressbrook Band was formed in 1881 and is one of the oldest village brass bands in the area. It is self-funding, raising money through subscriptions, concert fees and other fundraising activities. It is a non-competitive social band with about 28 members, most of whom live in the area and actively encourage local children to take up music, providing them with free tuition and free access to instruments. In a history of Cressbrook written in 1968 by Edward Sheldon, a resident of Cressbrook, he wrote:

"It is now a far cry (around 1881) since news reached the village that some instruments had arrived at

CRESSBROOK BRASS BAND.

Monsal Dale station. A body of men filled perhaps more with excitement than music rushed to the station, unpacked the instruments and to the station masters disgust departed leaving the platform covered in straw. The story is told how these chaps made their way home up the dale filling the air with a cacaphony of weird noises, so much so that some of Adam Mycocks sheep plunged into the river thinking that death was sweeter than that music. These first set of instruments cost £80"

Over many years since its formation the band has provided musical support for the village by playing at the many community group events

above: The torchlight parade, which is the finale of Gala Week
left: Cressbrook Brass Band in the late 1800s

happening throughout the year. In the summer they lead the procession through the village on Gala Day for a well-dressing blessing on the Green which is followed by a concert outside the Institute playing to villagers and visitors having afternoon tea and cakes. For the finale of Gala week, the band members head a torchlight parade around the village. Christmas in Cressbrook starts off with carol concerts in the Orangery at Cressbrook Hall, tickets sell out well in advance for this, two of the many carol concerts at which Cressbrook Band are invited to perform in surrounding villages.

There has been a longstanding tradition in the village for members of the band getting together on Christmas morning and working their way 'round the village playing seasonal tunes. For many years this would start at midnight of Christmas Eve with the sounds of *Christians Awake* echoing around Ravensdale but this now begins at 9.30am in Apprentice Row where another tradition of consuming sloe-gin, mulled wine and mince-pies with the residents has emerged. By no means a full turn-out and staffed by perhaps only half a dozen hardy souls, the show nonetheless gains the collective appreciation of all who witness it. Many in the past have expressed their considerable appreciation of the dedication and skill of the troubadours through the

above: Members of the band play carols in the snow on Christmas Day

left: Cressbrook Band in the 1960s

donation of copious amounts of strong spirit. Ostensibly to reinforce the players' extremities against the often cruel weather, the spirit inevitably has the associated effect of preventing the unwary and overindulgent from walking in a straight line or in extreme and well-documented cases from even

standing up. Starting at the bottom of the village at the mill on Christmas morning, over the next few hours the band works its way up the hill and despite the mulled wine, mince pies and other refreshments, eventually finishes at the Club at lunchtime for another opportunity to thaw out.

IN TUNE

*Together, **Ken Munns** and **Brian Bingham** have been playing in Cressbrook Band for nearly 105 years! Ken 'retired' two years ago but still plays and so does Brian*

Leading the torchlight parade at the end of Gala Week, Ken on E flat bass/tuba, Una Hill on trombone and Malcolm Burton also on trombone

KEN MUNNS

I first joined the band in 1947 and then I had a break probably for about five years and then I rejoined again in 1961. It was all from scratch when I started and learning the music was more difficult than anything - keeping up with it. One of the chaps would take you on one side and give you some lessons, mostly just scale-work more than anything. There'd be in the region of about 20, 22 in the band, they were all chaps out of the village at that time and we used to practice once a week, that was on a Sunday morning. I played a cornet in the first place, then I went on to baritone. Playing the instruments is just the same apart from playing in a different key or whatever and they were both B flat instruments. Now I'm on an E flat bass but the fingerings just the same for the notes. The other one I've been playing was what they call a double E flat and it's twice as heavy to hold as the other one. It's probably 70 years old and they don't increase in value with age as the metal gets thinner and thinner.

When I joined there was Horace Bingham as conductor and then Brian Bingham took over and we've had Helen Thurlby until this year but prior to Horace used to be Jack Willis and George Henry Robinson, they were before the war.

We used to go out to different carnivals around Tideswell, Stoney Middleton, Eyam, Great Longstone, Ashford. Used to do all parades round there and then we did concerts at Monsal Head, we would probably do a couple of concerts on a Sunday evening at Monsal Head. We didn't do a Christmas concert in those days, it's only just materialised over these last 10 years or something like that doing these regular concerts at Christmas.

We only do concerts and well-dressings and probably bits of carnivals and things and we don't do any contesting. At one time there were bands at most of the villages... there were always one at Tideswell same as Hathersage and Castleton - I mean they all had a band. Castleton, Hathersage and Tideswell are still going, and they'd one at Bakewell. We didn't do Ashford Well-dressings 2003 but we did do a concert in front of the Institute at Ashford and that was quite entertaining 'cos there was quite a lot of people about and ITV were down there doing a programme. It created a bit more interest rather than just sat there playing but the other concerts were always very entertaining and we always have a bit of fun.

Well, it used to be a family tradition in Cressbrook - I mean they all followed on from fathers and sons. Same as Willis family, I mean old Jack Willis where two of his lads went in, Graham and Fred. Fred finished up playing with Ransom & Miles, a big firm in Newark, used to make lawnmowers and things like that. They had a top class band and Fred went playing with them.

I retired two years ago but never actually finished. I regard myself as a guest player now and if they tell me they're short of a bass player I'll probably turn up, but I don't really want to feel as though I want to play at everything nowadays. You miss the outs, a bit of fun, we could always have some laughs.

If anybody wants to learn I would recommend it, you've got to be dedicated to a certain amount, but I think youngsters learn that they've got to practice and things like that.

If anybody wants to learn I would recommend it

A band of 26 members at Thornbridge Hall wearing the uniform paid for by Henry Boot of Thornbridge Hall pictured here with Mrs Boot. The band used to have to play concerts for Mr Boot as he would ring up, usually on a Friday night, requesting the band play on Saturday afternoon at the Hall. The drum is the one being used now with just the title changed to Cressbrook Band, not public band.

Jack and Victor Molloy in band uniform outside Middle Row

Members of Cressbrook Band performing at Thornbridge Hall, June 2005

BRIAN BINGHAM

I lived in Litton until I was seven but my father was a member of the band, my two uncles were members of the band and grandfather drummed so I'd known about the band for ever, but when I moved to Cressbrook in 1945 I actually joined as a learner, taught by a bloke called Horace Bingham who'd come back out of the RAF and had taken over conducting the band at that time. I started learning the cornet and I stayed on the cornet until I actually went into the band possibly 18 months later something like that. Then I went on to flugel horn, but only for a short time and went back on to cornet again and I'm still playing cornet at 66. My father played cornet, one of my uncles, Noel played cornet and the other uncle Edwin played tenor horn and Horace was my father's cousin. We celebrated the centenary of the band in 1980 so the band itself was going in 1880 which would be in my great grandfather's time I suppose.

We've always grown our own players sort of thing, taught them within the band, provided instruments for them and even when the people like my father's brothers and others families in the band, moved away to Tideswell or wherever, not too far away of course those days, but they all used to come back to rehearsals on a Sunday morning. They all used to come back on push bikes and but not the guy who played the euphonium, Edgar Gilbert, he lived in the village. There were two, three main families in the band at that time or before the war: Robinson's, Bingham's and Willis's. There weren't as many Ponsonby's in the band, there were some but there weren't as many and there was a big feud for years between the Robinson's and the Willis's. Now they were very well represented in the band, both families, but when one family was in after this feud - I've no idea what it was about - the other one was out and they wouldn't go to rehearsals. At one time George Henry Robinson conducted the band, back in the twenties or early thirties then the Willis's stayed away. Just before the war a bloke called Jack Willis took over as conductor of the band and the Robinson's stayed away. I think possibly the war was a very good thing as far as the band was

concerned because everybody played together again.

When I was in the RAF in '56 I played in the voluntary band at Binbrook and for a couple of years I conducted the voluntary band there. I was a sort of peripatetic band master who moved around all the area

Harriet and Chris Hulme with daughter Emily, play in the band as a family

Cressbrook Majorettes line-up at the Cressbrook Band Centenary 1981
left to right: Mandy Gratton, Angela Bingham, Julie Sharpley, Amanda Bingham, Louise Harland, Jacqueline Sharpley, Carol Bingham, Susan Oldfield

and just come in maybe once a fortnight to do the conducting. Horace Bingham, he came back out of the RAF '45 and conducted this band until '72. He didn't stamp any particular style of music on the band, they were probably still playing the stuff that they had been playing from the twenties and thirties which were more or less classical transcriptions which was what brass bands were playing at that time. Obviously brass bands go along with marches and so on and so forth, spend a lot of their time on their feet don't they. But I

>> *... brass bands go along with marches ... spend a lot of their time on their feet don't they...* ""

don't remember anything that I knew when I was young actually coming into the band as a brass band arrangement. I don't remember Horace bringing anything new in at all and when he died in '72 I took over then and packed up in 1993 I think it was - twenty one years. I got the choice of music as conductor and probably brought in a lot of new music. When I say 'new' music it was new music then, Beatles amongst other things. I had at that time played with both Tideswell and Cressbrook bands and I conducted both bands for a while, but I'd been with Tideswell since I was about 25 and of course played under various conductors. Tideswell was always a slightly different band in that Cressbrook

Brian conducting Cressbrook Band

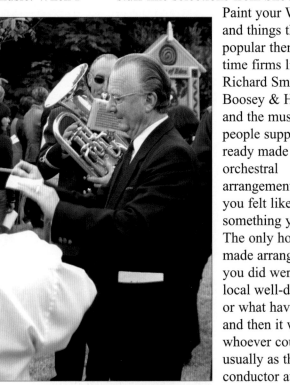

band the conductor was on a honorarium *(nominal sum)*. Tideswell always paid a professional conductor to come in and so they brought fresh music into the band. Having seen this, I'd seen how it worked better on concerts so when I took over Cressbrook band we brought in a lot of new music. Beatles, show music, stuff like selections from Showboat or Paint your Wagon and things that were popular then. At that time firms like Richard Smith, Boosey & Hawkes and the music people supplied ready made orchestral arrangements unless you felt like doing something yourself. The only home-made arrangements you did were for local well-dressings or what have you and then it was up to whoever could do it, usually as the conductor at the

Playing at the Great Longstone Festival in the 1950s and *below* at the Ashford-in-the-Water carnival

time you arranged them, but there wasn't a lot of light music around to arrange.

Helen Thurlby took over 1993 when I retired - I actually was ill, I got lung cancer so I had to pack up. Then I recovered and I went back blowing, but Helen took over in 1993 until retiring this year. Before that she played euphonium and was one of my pupils. There's just one difference made these last five, six years. A firm in Holland has blossomed, Bernaerts they're called, and he does a lot of popular, fairly simple music arrangements. They're in four parts, divided round the band and so Helen bought a lot of stuff from there

and the band play it out in concert in summer and it's been a very good thing for brass bands, it's allowed them to change their repertoire a great deal. Possibly until 1970ish all bands were male, we were all male. Only this year has one of the top bands taken a lady in on solo tenor horn, until then they were all male. When I took over the band it was male only, so I brought in learners - about seven learners in the first year. Girls I think it mainly was because I could see that by that time we weren't getting enough learners so I had to go looking elsewhere. I started off with my daughter and Gordon's daughter, Tony's daughter and Helen. They were all at school together and Philip my son - he now plays plays sop *(soprano cornet)* - were going to learn, so we got them all in at once. Like I say, we used to grow our own and we still do. Yes, there's a community feel.

Cressbrook Band in Litton 1977
back row l to r: Harold Redfern, Tony Bingham, Neil Spencer, Sam Bingham, Geoff Blackwell, Kevin Brabury, Raymond Mycock, Derk Skidmore, Brian Buckley, Pauline Ashmore, Stephen Mycock, Ronald Gainer
middle row l to r: Philip Bingham, Clive Gainer, Angela Bingham, A Ashmore, B Ashmore
front row l to r: Stuart Walker, Terrance Harrison, Ian Spencer, Helen Thurlby, Arthur Bingham, Brian Bingham, George Ponsonby, Gordon Sharpley, Ken Munns, Eddie Kenworthy, Alex Mycock, Rennie Robinson

But it also I think helps in shaping the way youngsters grow up because of the community style of the thing. They've another interest that seems to fire their minds a little.

"

97

A FARMERS BOY

Aubrey Howe farms at Litton Slack with his wife Elisabeth and son Tom. They explain how the fun has been pushed out of farming - pen-pushed by paperwork

" AUBREY AND ELISABETH HOWE

Our family has been at Litton Slack for about 62 years. My parents were born in Wardlow then went to live in a cottage down at Litton Slack before they bought Leisure Farm for £1200. Then it was a farmhouse, out buildings and 10 acres, but we've built it up and bought 145 acres of land since. My father only had a small-holding you see, 20 to 25 cows would be the most that they would milk but even then they were milked by machine. Dad died when he was 87, Mum was 76 and they're buried at Wardlow - they wanted to go back to Wardlow where they had been born.

We've built the farmhouse we live in now and it's a mixed farm - dairy, sheep and beef, but chiefly dairy, about 200 cows in total. Each day we milk towards 70 cows. The beef cattle are Simmental and Belgium Blue. The sheep are Texal Cross and the flock is about 65 head now.

After Cressbrook Primary and secondary school I left and worked at Home Farm, Cressbrook for about two years, then I did about six months in the mill which I hated. You're set on like an apprentice doing what they called *a layer on*, and what you did was you put the spindles between the cotton that was running for the doublers to *doff it off*, and the apprentice put these bobbins in for the doublers but I mean I absolutely hated it. And it was so hot, it was unreal in summertime. It wasn't my scene anyway but I mean a lot of the old doublers from Cressbrook you couldn't have dragged them out for anything, they absolutely loved it you know, that was their life really.

I did have a spell one very hot summer with my brother, building the raising of the mill pond dam wall with Arthur Barnes. Then I went to work down at Laportes mining. I did that and I sort of started building the farm up, getting more land together and then after that I went wagon-driving for a while. I was building the farm up, not making a living out of the farm but building it up money wise and we've got there you know. I have been married to Elisabeth for about 32 years and we've four children, two boys and two girls. Elisabeth contributes a lot to the farm. Apart from feeding them all, probably everyday, she does the accounts and Tom, my son who works the farm, does all the paperwork. The paperwork is horrendous. Passports for every cow and even sheep, yes, its horrendous. To be honest with you, I mean fair enough, if you wanted to do that kind of work you shouldn't have to be labouring like we're doing during the day. I mean that's somebody's job isn't it, it's a separate person's job.

PRESENT DAY FARMING

My son Tom helps on the farm and we have contract men come in to help us when we need, but other than that we do it ourselves. Farming's altered a terrific lot, there's no two ways about that, to what it was because you're having to keep more and more stock to make the same kind of return to what you were doing 25 years ago. Presently milk fetches about 17p a litre but it has been as good as 29p per litre when we sold to Nestlé, at Ashbourne. It went for evaporated milk and it used to go to Third World countries, but when foot and mouth and BSE came it killed the trade and those countries wouldn't buy anymore of Nestlés, that's why the factory shut. Now our milk goes all over the country: we sell to First Milk and it can end up at the Westbury Plant where they make skimmed milk, powdered milk, cheese, whatever. Every day there's tests taken on the milk and we've got bactoscan cell counts, butter fat protein, lactose, everything really. And if it isn't up to the quality you'd be on even less

" *The paperwork is horrendous. Passports for every cow and even sheep, yes, its horrendous* "

money – in fact in some cases you could be down to a penny a litre if it wasn't up to the quality that they want. These tests have built up pretty quick actually, over the last five year maybe. I mean before they used to take milk to Longstone Station in churns and there was an old guy there used to just pull the lid up and smell at it; if it smelt sweet it went, if it was sour it came back.

The milk board wagon comes just once a day. Originally, when we were with Nestlé's, they used to come every other day because they were manufacturing and it didn't matter to them about it. Some of this milk you know in all honesty it'll be two or three days old before it's even bottled, which I think is wrong. I mean you know they heat it up and pasteurise it

> ## " When we first started farming it was adventurous but now there's so much red tape and form filling "

and so the milk won't go sour now, but it'll go rotten.

When we first started farming it was adventurous, but now there's so much red tape and form filling. It's not just peoples attitude towards you, but the ministry's attitude as well. The ministry, now they're not helpful by a long, long way.

Elisabeth: "When we first started you could make something of it if you tried really hard. You could go forward and you could get somewhere if you

wanted to get somewhere but now you're just knocking your head against a brick wall whatever you try, you can't get on."

Aubrey: In past people come and tell you if there was something wrong or something got out, now I think they just run it down or whatever. I think people don't want to get involved. Peak Park came to me and they said we've got some land on right to roam. Fortunately I've appealed against it and I've got it (right to roam) off. He said I hope your insurances are up to date 'cos if anybody gets injured on there you're liable.

No, you're not in control really. I don't think a lot of people appreciate the amount of time and effort that goes into looking after stock. It's a way of life isn't it really, its more than a job isn't it? Not just when you fancy, not Monday to Friday. You've still got milking at weekends.

They're that used to going into a supermarket now and there's such a wide choice isn't there? I mean its unreal to what it was, even in our time, and they don't realise where it's come from you know. In the past everybody

John and Aubrey Howe

A prize bull with no name, just a number

had hencotes and hens and your children would see it. I was lucky, we'd some little chickens hatched out and me grandson was up and I took him down when this little chicken was just coming out of its egg. I think its lovely for them to see nature.

When they're lambing we bring the sheep inside. We turn the tups out on about October 25th. We used to turn out on November 5th so the lambs come on April 1st, but now we've brought them forward for this last few years, so they start lambing about March 20th. We made it earlier so we can get them lambed and footed and moved away from the farm, so we've got the spring grass coming for the milk cows round the farm. Every year on average we get about 115 lambs. We sell them at Bakewell market. The price of lamb last year would average about 50 apiece 'cos of export but without export you wouldn't get owt like that price.

I mean we're fortunate that we only take our cows and sheep down to Bakewell. You see the trouble is they've done away with all these small abattoirs. They have all been centralised and you see Redferns only kill the BSE cows now. We do have one or two slaughtered for our own personal use, we take them to Butterton which is a fair run to what Bakewell was. I can remember a time we came into Bakewell one summer and it must have been market day 'cos it was absolutely packed. And then Nelsons the pork butchers - they was very good butchers up Buxton road – they had a little slaughter house with grey doors just on the other side from the fire station and he used to run the pigs up from Bakewell market. I can see him taking them up now, into this little building to store them over night and kill them on the Tuesday and, like

Texal cross sheep and lambs

> *the first lot of land I bought I gave hundred pound an acre for it and me dad said I'd give too much*

we were saying, really that was better. Yes I mean that's what I can't just understand, the ministry shutting down all these small slaughter houses. There was a local farmer who'd got offered a really good contract for his beef from a major supermarket chain, it was somewhere in the midlands, but he turned it down in the end because he said it was far too many miles for his animals to be driven to the slaughter house. No, I just think its such an unnecessary stress on the beasts. I don't think I'd encourage children to go into farming. I mean I know Tom likes it and me young son likes it, but he's not going to go into farming. I think if we had us time to go again, we wouldn't have encouraged Tom to but he likes it anyway. He's going on holiday for a week but he's had to do a lot of work prior as there's nobody else. Elisabeth says when we kicked off doing it there was a way

forward and we wanted to do that, now you are just bogged down, you're not in your own destiny really which is wrong. It's the red tape that's come along with this government isn't it? We've a small piece on with English Nature which has got an SSSI (site of special scientific interest) sign in it. It's for the hawthorns and grasses and cowslips, but there's no primroses now. It's on the Slack as you go down the Dark Lane, it runs down where the field that's never been grazed is in the bottom.

FARMING HISTORY

The first lot of land I bought I gave £100 an acre for it and me dad said I'd give too much. There'll only be a few farms left nearby now: there's Gregory's, Weston's, Des Hall. In Litton, they'll be three farms left now where there was about 10.
I remember years ago my mum and dad used to make black pudding; everybody had pigs then. After the war they used to keep two or three pigs and you were allowed one for yourself and the other the ministry took to feed the country. That was the

law - to get corn I can remember having coupons.
After the war for whatever you wanted to buy there was a lot of swapping. My Dad did with the pigs, there were dentists and the bloke that used to sell the clothes at Buxton, they were both money people but they couldn't get hold of pigs, so Dad used to fix them up.
The pig killing was on a Saturday morning as I remember. They used to do them and this guy, Fred Furniss used to come, he was a slaughterman and a butcher and he used to do it for a lot of people, 'cos everybody used to keep the odd pig and hens and have allotments. I mean at the back of the church there was all allotments down there, so everybody was sort of self sufficient. You couldn't go into a supermarket in them days and just pick up whatever you wanted. We had this big boiler, a 45 gallon drum with a fire under to boil the water so he could scrape the pig and get all the hairs off it and you'd be doing an hour and a half of it you know, cleaning this pig.
He used to come back few weeks after and put the salt on it to preserve it; salting was a labourer's job to do.
Then they used to hang the hams and the bacon up to go really rock hard, the hanging did the trick and it would keep

like that for months and months. I suppose really when you think back it was very fatty, but very tasty.

From one pig we could make a fair lot of black pudding I remember. We used to stir it and get the things, clots, out. And my mother used to make brawn and all that and obviously make too much for one family to eat so we used to give it to relations. And also you'd got pantries and cool places, cellars which you haven't got now and I suppose it did keep better in them kind of places. I remember after the war that if you went out to see anybody you always took with you not a bunch of flowers or something, you actually took a pint of milk and some eggs. And every Christmas he used to be doing these chickens for relatives.

Years ago I can remember Joe Harrison telling how three men used to mow a three and a half acre field by scythe, they used to get up at half past four in the morning, mow till it got too hot and then start again the following day. He used to hand-milk these four cows and they used to have a can and pint measure and I remember him going round Pilsley near Bakewell and he used to measure you out a pint of milk you know. **"**

BLACK PUDDING RECIPE
from Philip Gibb, NT Gibbs Tideswell Butchers
Source: *Handy Guide for Pork Butchers by Thomas Finney. Printed 1908*

Ingredients:
14 lbs Groats or pearl barley
10 lbs of leaf or back fat
7 lbs Flour or fine oatmeal
3 lbs Onions
3 lbs Farina (usually potato flour)
4 gallons of pork blood
12 oz salt
7 oz pepper
4 oz Bergice

Flavouring: *North Staffordshire*
4 lbs rubbed marjoram
4 lbs thyme
2 lbs pennyroyal
3 lbs ground pimento
2 lbs coriander

1 Take the barley, tie loosely in a bag and boil until cooked. Put cooked barley in a tub and add seasoning, flour and onions and mix well together whilst hot.
2 Add 10lbs fat cut into inch squares, allow to stand until fat warmed. Add blood and stiffen with farina and oatmeal.
3 Put mixture into bullock runners *(intestines)* or wide hog *(sheep)* castings *(intestines)* with a pudding filler *(looks like wide funnel)*.
4 Allow 4 pieces fat to each pudding. Tie up firmly and boil gently for 20 min.

PLEASE NOTE: This is not Phil's secret award winning recipe. Norman has forbidden him to tell anyone!

LEISURE FARM

Just above the village of Cressbrook, on the road to Litton, there is a farm built next to a stand of beautiful beech trees below a sharp, precipitous and windswept corner. The views from here are stunning, reaching is far in the west as the Cat and Fiddle near Shining Tor and in the south as far as Crich Stand. It is called Leisure Farm and it takes its name from the corner in the road which has been called Leisure Corner since the days when William Newton was master at Cressbrook Mill and Ellis Needham was master at Litton Mill. The peculiar name is derived from the fact that this is the furthest point in the road from Cressbrook that the apprentices of the mill were allowed to venture 'at their leisure'. At this time there was no through road to Litton and the unmade track was barred by a gate but despite the upgrading of the track to a through road and the removal of the physical barrier, the spirit of the place remains through its name.

BORN'n BRED

*Going to school, working in the mill, being the school caretaker and then the postmistress. Enthusiasm overflows from **Carol Harland's** memories of living in Cressbrook*

"

CAROL HARLAND

I was born at Litton Slack so my first recollection was a very basic and very small community because there was the three of my sisters and the only other children down there was the Tibbles, so there were two boys and that was my first life really which was lovely. I went to Cressbrook School and I think I was four or four and a half and I can remember going the first day. We walked to New Houses, my eldest sister was going to Tideswell School then so I walked up with her. I can remember going on the bus which brought us down to Cressbrook School and then she went on to Tideswell School and I pulled the teacher's hair, not on purpose but I was holding on to the back of the seat at the time and I pulled her hair. It was Andrew's Buses, it was a school bus only and they used to pick me up and take me to school and drop me off again at night time and I'd walk down the lane. I never remember the bad days. I can remember lovely spring days walking up the lane, I don't know why but that's my recollection of it. There were 20 in the class when I was little with children from Cressbrook or Litton Mill because Litton Mill School was closed by then, so there were quite a few of them 'cos our family was six and then the Allens they had five or six children, but my best friend, she lived on Top Row and lived with her

Marie Howes interviewing Carol *right*

Grandma. We had about seven different teachers while I was there from four to 11. It was weird because you had the infant teacher and then you had one what did the juniors and in total there were seven different women, they was all women as well. We had one lady called Mrs Wildgoose and she actually lived on Dale Terrace. She bought a cottage down there when she was a teacher and it was the house I went to live in when I got married. But she was a fantastic teacher, did very good things.

My first teacher was Mrs Stubbs, oh she was a huge lady, she looked absolutely enormous to me and she came from Buxton and her daughter was the infant teacher at the time. I must admit it was daunting to start school especially with that teacher, but I loved Cressbrook School. When you're in a junior school it's the main part of your life, you used to go to school, you used to come home and you used to play, it was brilliant. It was just two teachers who really stood out to us. Mrs Stubbs, I wouldn't say she was a brilliant teacher, she was far from it, but Mrs Wildgoose she was better, she brought new ideas with her. She sticks in my mind a lot, the others they just came and went. Then I went to Tideswell School.

Being in a church school connected to Tideswell Church I used to go down and sing a lot in the choir at Tideswell Church. The vicar there was called Mr Rice and he was always ringing the school asking, 'Can you just send Carol down' and I used to go and think what does he want me for now and he'll say, 'Right you can do a reading for us at Easter.' I used to dread it honestly, I didn't like reading and when it was Christmas they used to get to the Nine lessons and Carols and the music teacher always picked *A Virgin Most Pure* and I used to have to sing the first verse up in the chancel so she used to say, 'Well if I give you a few aspirins it'll calm your nerves for you and you'll be alright!' I used to go to church regularly at Cressbrook, always have done. We had a Sunday School and I used to go to that and Mr Bingham, Horace Bingham, he was the verger of Cressbrook Church and he started the choir so there was about eight of us in the choir for Cressbrook which was brilliant really because they hadn't had a choir for ages. We used to go and practice on a Thursday night in the church what we were going to sing for the following Sunday and in those days we used to have to sing the psalms as well as the hymns.

My dad had done farming virtually all his life in Wardlow where he was brought up and my mum, her father was a farmer in Wardlow so they've always had connections with farming, and they bought Leisure Farm and we all moved up there. It was such a big

> ## *If the mill hadn't closed I would have been working there now, definitely, because I loved it* "

house from a little cottage, it was huge but the funny thing was it had no running water and it had no electricity. We had a big tank under the sitting-room floor with a big pump on the sink and you pumped the water out, it was rain water and the actual lights downstairs was gas and upstairs you had candles, fascinating because we'd been used to having electricity.

The title Leisure Farm was for the leisure of apprentices at the mill, they could go as far as that and no further and back down again, but it's a funny name really for a farm isn't it, leisure? The time came to leave school and my music teacher thought that as I've

always been interested in children I was going to be the singing nanny. I don't know if she thought I was Mary Poppins or what but yes, she used to say right I can imagine you as a singing nanny. My oldest brother and sister got me a job down at the mill. I didn't go for an interview, I'd not thought about it much, I did think about working with children, definitely I did, but in those days you came out of school and you went straight to the mill. Everyone had gone to the mill, either to Litton Mill or they'd gone to the cotton mill down at Cressbrook and my brother and sister automatically asked was there any jobs going. I was a reeler when I first went, there weren't many of them. You had these bobbins of cotton and you made them into great big hanks of cotton. It was like a hexagon machine what went round with struts, which kept it in position, and you got so

Carol with brother Aubrey and puppies at Leisure Farm

much weight of the cotton on to this machine and then you had to thread your fingers through and then thread some more cotton through the other way and tie them together every so often to keep the hanks of cotton in place and then you put them on long poles. There was only about five of us what actually did it in the whole mill, all the others did other jobs. I did that for quite a while, then they wanted me to learn how to do coning in case anyone were off ill or sick.

This was on more modern machines - the actual reeling machine was absolutely antiquated. I've not seen nothing like it, it was so old-fashioned but these coning machines were the bee's knees, quite modern. There was only two ladies who did that - it was quite a selected few you know but I learnt to do that. I made the cones which were not made of wood, it was like compressed cardboard. So it came off a bobbin, a wooden bobbin and it came off and went on to these big cones. There's special knots you used to have to tie and set it off on the cone and you used to have to keep your eye on it. You had a measuring stick and you used to have to measure them and as they got to a certain size you had to stop it and put a new one on because the measure told you how thick the cotton had got, the weight and what have you, fascinating really. Then they said, right we'll show you to do another job so I went into the cop-winding and that's very similar but you don't put them onto cones you put

them on the normal wooden bobbin off the long ones, on to a shorter one and it was a round shape. That's when I really met Vera because she worked at the other side of the machine to me, she was a good workmate at the other side. If the mill hadn't closed I would have been working there now, definitely, because I loved it, absolutely loved it at Cressbrook Mill. I met Dick at the mill when he came to work there. I can't remember him at school in Tideswell but I can remember his friends quite vividly, a lot of the boys who he used to go about with I can remember, I can't remember Dick at all, very weird. And Aubrey, one of my brothers, he was working at the mill as well and it was one evening, it was a gorgeous summer's evening and they was playing football I think down in the mill field, 'cos the mill field was for doing games and things and they were playing football and I was there and I met Dick. If he hadn't have started going about with Aubrey I don't think I'd have ever met him probably, I don't know, but that's how I met him. The job he was doing at the mill was, oh gosh what do you call it, yes he was *duggling*. Don't ask me what it entails because I didn't really know. I did go down to have a look but it looked... it was always very greasy. Oh it was terrible, a very dirty job. Then the mill closed just before we were married. It started that there wasn't as much work about, you could tell, the yarn was dropping off so you didn't have a full machine and what have you. Then the rumours started going round that it was going to have to close. So my eldest sister and I, she said 'Right if its going to close we'll have to look for another job,' so we did. We went and looked and the first job we went to we was only there a week. It was horrible and he didn't actually pay us for what he said the women was getting so we weren't very happy about that. So we went up to Thornbridge Hall, it was a teacher training place and we did sewing, preparing meals for the students, everything, whatever wanted doing and Dick went up to Glebe Mines. My brother John stayed on at the mill, he never finished when it actually closed from the cotton and Kays bought it, and I don't know what they actually did down there. They used to store a

lot of things like a warehouse place so he was down there for quite a while John was.

It was a shame because you used to be quite connected to Tideswell, you know and the people who used to come in you got friendly with them. There were some really old ladies, well they was old to me, they looked old but they lived quite a way after the mill closed so they mustn't have been as old as I was thinking, but it was a shame to lose contact with them. We got married in Tideswell Church and I didn't sing that time I'd got laryngitis. So I'd virtually got no voice at all and Dick was really ill because he used to have tonsillitis virtually every fortnight and the doctor said, 'If we don't get your tonsils out you might have rheumatic fever and you're going to be really ill.' So when we got married it really should have been cancelled, but the doctor gave him an injection on the morning we got married and it lasted through the day. When we knew we were going to get married Dick said 'Where are we going to live?' and I said 'Certainly not Tideswell.' I went to school, I went to church, I've done a lot of things in Tideswell but I wouldn't like to live there so I said 'We'll live at Cressbrook.' It was by chance we heard that Mr and Mrs Grant was moving from 6 Dale Terrace so I said well we'll go and have a look. Next door was Mrs Goodwin, Vera's auntie

Carol and Dick outside Tideswell Church

> ## " *it was like moving into a family and they were brilliant, absolutely brilliant neighbours* "

and there was Mrs Worsencroft and Peter and his dad and there was Arthur Barnes who I knew from working at the mill. I knew Mrs Worsencroft 'cos she was a cop winder as well, so I knew them all on the row, so I said yeah, I could live here. So off we went to Stanton Estates and we met Mr Davies and he said 'Yes, there's a house coming up for grabs, are you interested?' and Dick said yes. He said 'Well if you take it you take it on what it is, you don't come back and say it hasn't got a water toilet, it hasn't got this, it hasn't got the other, you take it as it is and you can have it for ten shillings a week,' so we got it. Well its so little but I guess in them days I was earning £11 a week, I can't remember what Dick was earning but I was earning £11 that was in 1966 or 1967, so we said yes, we'd have it. So we have to start decorating and my eldest sister who was good at wallpapering came and helped and got it ready for us to move in when we got married. I knew them all on the row because we all worked down at the mill. Right at the end there was Mrs Smith. Margaret Smith's the same age as my eldest sister so I knew them all on that row. It was like moving into a family

virtually and they were brilliant, absolutely brilliant neighbours, really were and I thoroughly enjoyed living there. I was there for about 17 years and it was a lovely place to live. We had such laughter it was brilliant, you never locked your doors, you used to go shopping, you used to go to work, used to do everything, you never locked a door on Dale Terrace. Cressbrook's like two separate villages, I know it shouldn't be, but it was, it really was. Living at both ends of the village now, I can see the divide you know and it's a shame because they were lovely people and I don't really know them now down there, there's only Arthur and Vera who I really know.

When Dick saw this land up here for sale he said I've always wanted to build my own house it would be really good. He was working for David at Cressbrook Mill which involved building and I think David probably encouraged him more than anything to buy the land. David had bought the mill and moved in while we was at Dale Terrace and David had got a daughter around the same age as Louise, so they got friendly and Mark tried to get friendly with the twins but

Above, back row: Mary Howe, Helen Brown, A.Yates, Jan Lewis, Carmen Gaynor, Tom Howe, *front row:* Nicola Harland, Harriet Hulme, B. Yates, Ann-Marie Houghton, Emma Longson, Donna Longson, Sarah Hoare, Cassie Longson

right: Cressbrook Morisettes

they were just that little bit older but he used to go and play with them. We moved up the hill in 1981 yes, moved up from the works to the better quality of life. I don't think I'd have moved up quite so quick if it hadn't have been for Mrs Thorpe. One day she'd seen Dick building the new house and she'd gone to him and she said 'Will you tell Carol to call in, I want a word with her.' I'd known Mrs Thorpe all my life, she used to give me sweets and that, so off I trotted one day and she says 'Do you fancy doing the Post Office?' I said certainly not, she said 'Why not?' I said 'Oh no, all them forms, oh no its not me.' She said 'It is. You're the only one I can think of, there's only you I think I dare

trust.' I said 'Yeah go on then.' She said 'Right I'll put your name forward.' We started the Post Office in our house in 1981 and that's why I moved up quicker than I should have done. Mr Bird used to come every day from Stockport to train me when we first started doing the post and, gosh, I did it for 20 years and before that I was the school caretaker as well, I forgot about that. The job come up for grabs there so Mrs Daykin said 'If you want to apply you can apply' which I did and I did that for about 24 years. I got involved with the school a lot working there because when it was Christmas or they was doing plays I used to do costumes with the teachers. Or when they was going on a field study day they used to come and say 'Oh Carol would you like to come with us and bring so many children.' So off we used to toddle on different voyages. Then when the school started to go

down-hill with numbers we had meetings and got involved in saving the school twice. I went to London with a group from the village to give the village perspective of the school. When my children were younger, there was myself, Pat and Lynne especially, we used to get together and we did all sorts with our children because with them all being in the same age group they got on so well. We started doing majorettes with the little ones, now they was little, I think Cathy and Nicola and Sarah, I think they were around two, two and a half, and we used to do rehearsals with them up at the church and down Dark Lane, oh it was incredible, we had, oh it was, I can't explain - the atmosphere was electric. It was absolutely brilliant. The music was from a cassette, we did it to modern music mostly, I can't think what it was called, a right jazzy tune we used to have then.
Also, I don't know how it came about but we said what about entering into the Wakes at Tideswell because we'd got quite a group of young ones you know. So we wondered what we going to take them on 'Well what about your Aubrey, do

you think he'd have a tractor and trailer we could use?' Then Mary and Tom, 'cos they lived on the Top Row did the tractor and trailer for us and he used to bring it down and put it on our drive and we used to wash it off and decorate it. We got a prize for *Alice in Wonderland* that year. We used to go from Cressbrook on Saturday afternoon, arrive at two o'clock for the judging then off we went. I used to walk right round Tideswell with them on the trailer, we did *Liquorice Allsorts* one year which was brilliant. Its like Gala Day, they asked us what can we bring into the Gala Day to make it different, so we said 'Well we've got all these young children, what about fancy dress? We'll dress them all up and parade them by the band and we'll have them judged.' So we started doing that.

"

105

Life in Cressbrook

To those people who live in big cities where social events are available all the time, village social life - especially in a small village - may appear to be non-existent

A suitably steep piece of newly-mown grass for the Easter egg-rolling competition

below: The many variations of decorating an Easter egg by young Cressbrookians

Without a conscious effort from the local residents, for much of the time between the end of October and the beginning of March Cressbrook can appear to be the Marie Celeste of the Peak. A dark, misty, crewless ship with just an occasional glimpse of a person perhaps hiding behind a wall or half sighted disappearing between two houses, sometime just after sunrise or just before dark. It is around this time that the importance to the village of the social club is highlighted, offering a focus for the village and giving people good reason to venture away from the warmth of the fireside. This period also emphasises the importance of community spirit as, were it not for the people who are prepared to put in their own time and effort to arrange events at the club then surely we would all stay by that warm fireside and the sense of community would no doubt perish in the winter cold. While the existence of the Entertainments Committee at the club is widely known in the village, it nonetheless comes as a pleasant surprise when the announcement of an up and coming event arrives either in the form of a slip of paper through the door, posters pinned up around the village or in a flyer tucked inside the fortnightly delivery by Ken and Vera Munns of the *Peak Advertiser*. Regular events at the club now include a folk music night once a month, quiz nights - with only occasional questions on nuclear physics - world music nights and a monthly film night arranged by the village film club with screenings of old, new and foreign films. A grant to purchase the screen, projector and sound equipment came from Awards for All (a lottery grant available for local groups) and Derbyshire Community Foundation. And a book-reading group has been formed for those who like to read and discuss books which others recommend, are best-sellers or award winners.

CRESSBROOK ART SHOW

May has recently seen the establishment of the Cressbrook Art Show, which from humble beginnings in 2001 with only twenty one pieces on show has grown steadily with over sixty pieces displayed in 2004's event. Over 50 percent of the pictures in the show come from local residents while the catchment from the remainder is kept as local as possible with artists from Great Longstone and Ashford-in-the-Water being regular invitees. The future seems bright for the show and plans are in motion to

Gareth Watkins, *left:* chairman of Cressbrook Club presents a member of the Ragged Trousered Mountaineering Club with a long-service certificate for taking their annual reunion holiday here for 20 years and taking part in the produce auction

far left: Admiring the entries
left: Ron Hill booking in the entries
left: Critical judging of the exhibits
below: Guy Buckley getting into his stride as auctioneer

expand the scope of the show and its duration in the coming years.

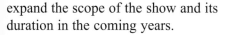

One of the larger exhibits in the art show

PRODUCE SHOW

Toward the end of August the village acquires an uncharacteristic air of competitiveness with usually friendly neighbours throwing covetous looks at the state of the vegetables and flowers in the gardens next door. It is once again time for the Cressbrook Produce Show, where the best and finest of the edible and inedible are laid out for judgement in the hopes of gaining recognition and plaudits for the skill of their growers and makers. Tomatoes, runner beans, potatoes and onions,

jam, fancy cakes and sponge cakes line up next to bunches of flowers and a new section for arts and crafts. All submissions should be registered before 12am at the Club and for two agonising hours the proud owners are forced to sit out under the shade of the gazebo enjoying ale and wine while the judges taste a few of the entries

and pass a hypercritical eye over the fruit, vegetables, arts and crafts. Then, after 2pm the competitors are re-admitted to the room to find where in the pantheon of vegetable greatness their creations have been placed and what riches have been lavished upon them. Perhaps 20p for a second place or even a 'not placed' in a field of only two runners. Even a first place in a field of one is flaunted proudly. While the show itself is always a source of friendly competition and boundless entertainment, it is only a forerunner of the day's main event, which happens in the club in the evening when the entries for the show are auctioned off for charity. Under the influence of alcohol and the skill and guile of Guy Buckley, the auctioneer aided by 'Samantha', the audience are encouraged to part with truly astronomical sums for even the humblest parsnip or buttonhole. The

55 runners, experienced and first-timers lined up for the inaugural Cressbrook Crawl Fell Race, a new event through the limestone valley of the river Wye and over the hills of the White Peak. The winner completed the 6.5 mile course, in 45 minutes.

top left: Cheese and Wine evening
left: Gondwana - world music night
below: Place your bets - its Race Night!

best cakes demand very high prices with furious bidding wars breaking out for choice chocolate sponges while almost inevitably there is a glut of huge remainder marrows at the end of the evening which go for a song to anyone with the will and the funds to take them. It is all immense fun and towards the best possible causes.

RACE NIGHT

Just how much fun can a group of party-minded people have with six small, wooden horses and a bag of bingo tokens ? Tears of laughter and rage typify Race Night at Cressbrook Club. Each race comprises six horses, each a different colour, moving along

'Land of Hope and Glory' - and its the Last Night of the Proms at Cressbrook Club and time for flag waving

Cressbrook Time *(noun)* A peculiar temporal paradox local to a small corner of Derbyshire (UK) in which time ceases to exhibit the rigid patterns of the real universe and instead adopts unpredictable irregularity. To an observer subject to Cressbrook Time, events expressed and measured in real universe time do not appear to commence or finish in a predictable fashion.

rails across a board marked in squares. The first horse to reach the right hand side of the board is the winner. The bingo tokens, drawn from the bag by members of the audience, determine which horse moves along the board. Cash is placed for notional but highly competitive bets and each horse in the race is bought and named by a member of the audience, with both owner of the winning horse and

successful punters collecting their winnings. Six races are held together with a seventh, a winners race, where all of the winners from the previous races meet for a final showdown and grand prize ... a bottle of wine! The end of the evening leaves all of the participants exhausted while the horses are brushed down and boxed up for a year.

OAPs CHRISTMAS PARTY

It has been a longstanding tradition in the village for members of the Cressbrook Community Association to put on a Christmas meal for the older residents of the community. Jan

Jeff Perks, Carol Harland and Jane Money contribute their 'wishes' to the Parish Plan on 'Wish List' Day. Parish Plans aim to help village communities develop their own futures. Top of the list was building improvements to Cressbrook Club followed by landscaping of the village green and providing wheelchair access, more facilties for the increased number of children now living in the village, a residents parking scheme, more public transport and a speed limit through the village.

Hallowe'en. An excuse for dressing up to frighten people by the younger villagers at a party held in the Club

Cressbrook Band waggling their reindeer antlers at the annual Christmas concert in the Club

Una and Ron Hill with Paul Radcliffe proudly display a grant cheque for the desperately needed restoration of the club roof

Christine Fielding begins clearing out the rooks nests which have been occupying the club attic

Watkins takes over the kitchen while other members of the village help out, scurrying back and forth to deliver a feast; sherry to start followed by a bowl of soup. Then comes a full-on Christmas dinner complete with turkey while plum pudding and trifle are hot on its heels. Nor does it stop there, as waiting in the wings is Christmas cake, cheese course, coffee and biscuits. Is it any wonder that we don't see some of the older residents again until Gala Day?

BOXING DAY WALK

Nobody is really sure whether the Boxing Day walk is born out of the guilt of overindulgence or the boredom of Christmas television. It is up to the individuals to find their own motives but nought but the worst of winter weather prevents the assembly of a good crowd outside the club just before lunch on Boxing Day to make the pilgrimage to the Anglers Rest in Millers Dale, some two miles away. A quick imbibement interrupts the

exercise before everyone retraces their steps to return to the club, where a bowl of hot soup is the perfect antidote to the winter chill.

A working party from the Community Group, clearing up the car-park area

Remembrance Day in Cressbrook is commemorated by a service in the church of St John the Evangelist accompanied by Cressbrook Band, followed by a march to the War Memorial in Middle Row where a wreathe is laid.

PAT KELLY

Miss Goodwin got engaged to a fighter pilot and when he was on leave he used to pick her up at the school. We used to giggle about the way they looked at each other and then one day she told us she was getting married and when she came back we were to call her Mrs Brett. She was blushing like mad, we all thought it was so romantic. I cant remember when, but somebody came to the school one day to see Mrs Brett and we saw she was very white and crying and we were let home early. The next day we had a temporary teacher who stayed quite a few days. We were told Mrs Bretts fighter pilot husband had been shot down and presumed dead in Germany.

GARY PITCHFORD

We used to share our camp (in Iraq) with Norwegians 'cos there was all sorts in the camp, there were Danes, Germans, some Italians, Czechs and there was like a dozen internet stations you could use.They're open 24 hours and you could go on and just sit there

for as long as you like and because of the nature of everybody's duties meant that some people they came off duty at 2 o'clock in the morning they'd use it then, so there was very rarely a queue, and you could access more or less any site in the world. Steve Morrison at the Mill, he came up with a website of the place and I used to log onto that as there were plenty of pictures and a great one actually looking at my apartment. So while other people were looking on the dating agency sites and auto trader about what bike they're going to buy when they get back or car, I'd be zooming in on the Mill pictures - quite literally I could see the windows of my flat. I don't know

if I suffered homesickness, I mean I don't know what the definition of it is, if you're missing home yes, I wanted to be home many times. We talk about the Cressbrook bubble being down here and the fact that you don't really have to leave the village but out there I was in sort of like the military bubble where nothing else really mattered and so it was nice to view things that were green. As you can see in some of the pictures, everything is just sand and if you go a little bit further North there's the marsh lands. Some of the land is plush and green, but it's a very flat sort of country, so there are no hills or valleys, nothing like that.

WHY I LIKE LIVING IN CRESSBROOK

CONNOR LONGSON - AGE 9
I like living in Cressbrook because there is no vandalism and all the children are nice. I love the beautiful views everywhere you look. In the summer I like going on long walks, picking blackberries then eating them. When winter comes we have snowball fights and make snowbases and snowmen. When we get cold we go home for hot chocolate.
Most of all I love Cressbrook because it is very quiet and peaceful.

ALICE & MAX SAVAGE - AGE 7 & 5
Alice: All I can think of is that I love living in Cressbrook. It's great, no other village in Derbyshire is like Cressbrook. It's so peaceful. When you come into the village you don't hear noisy motorbikes, you hear birds chirping. Everyone knows each other and we are all good friends. All the neighbours are very kind to us and so are the other people in the village ('not all of them' interjects Max).

Max: You can get to the village green without going on the road from Paul and Chris's garden.There's a secret passage through the undergrowth and there's nettles and weeds that stick out.
Alice: We have parties in the club, Christmas parties, birthday parties and Hallowe'en and at Easter we decorate eggs and have competitions.
Max: In Cressbrook its sad sometimes and happy sometimes. Nature dies and nature grows.
Alice: There's lot of animals and birds to watch and buds break open in the spring. When I'm lying in bed at night I can hear the owl hooting

HELENA STEPHENS - AGE 6¾
I like riding my bike in the hills and playing with my friends. Love Helena

Gala Week

This week is the one time that it is guaranteed that all of the people who live in the village, either turn out to help or attend the Gala Day itself

Gala Day attracts large numbers of visitors, many of which have long-standing connections with Cressbrook through friends, family or work. Some are also returning to the place where they spent much of their lives, such is the strong bond that Cressbrook grows with the people who live here.

There is a long record of community gatherings in Cressbrook, which while inevitably not as long-established as in older villages, are nonetheless key social events. While the mill was still operating there were events to coincide with Wakes Week, which were funded and organised by the mill owners. It is evident from photographic history as well as personal testimony that Cressbrook Hall was the focus for such occasions, with all and sundry turning out in their best

Cressbrook Band marching through the village - and its the start of Gala Week

clothes to attend. In living memory there are recollections of summer events at the Hall as far back as 1959, with hog roasts and games on the lawn. The break with this tradition came in the late seventies with the Queen's Silver Jubilee. People from Cressbrook had long been attending Tideswell for the Gala there and as the progressive changing hands of the ownership of Cressbrook Hall somewhat eroded its patriarchal role so the people of the village took inspiration from Tideswell and set about creating their own Gala. The Cressbrook Community Group was formed later that year and in 1979, two years after the seeds of the idea were first sown, Cressbrook had its first Gala. The embryonic Cressbrook Gala was a small affair in which some games were played, there was a fun-run from Litton to Cressbrook, the band entertained and a party was held at the club. Over the succeeding years,

however, the Community Group became more and more ambitious and now Gala lasts the entire week. Still within the itinerary are those events that started it all off; games, the band and a party but these are now just part of a much larger programme that includes the creation of a well dressing, many stalls set along the road outside the club, live music and other entertainments at the club during the course of the week. Early attempts to expand the Gala into its present form almost met with disaster. An advertisement spot on BBC Radio Derby for the first present-format Gala produced a huge response and the village was barely able to cope with the influx of visitors. This was exacerbated by the fact that, not having foreseen the response, The Community Group had not made any plans to have the road through the village closed off. Thronging crowds thus filled the road while at the same

111

The Dads-sack-race.

time frustrated motorists struggled in vain to progress through the crowds. The tea stall could not keep pace with the demand for refreshments and many visitors went home unimpressed. The Community Group took stock of that day and all subsequent Gala Days have been accompanied by a road closure. The peace and tranquility that the car-free road delivers only further enhances the magical and special air that the happiness of the day itself creates. The events which make up Gala week are complex and it is beyond the energies of any individual to make it happen. It is thus with great credit to the village that Gala continues to be popular. The role of the Community Group in this is key. The Group does not have any fixed membership beyond the committee, which itself gets reorganised every year when the elections come around. The committee

advertises the Community Group meetings and all those people in the village who have an interest in them attend. The meetings associated with Gala Week are invariably better attended than others, such is the measure of care within the community for the special week. In the spring at planning meetings, volunteers put their names forward for the jobs which comprise the preparation for Gala Day and the Gala Day events themselves. Appeals for volunteers are made to the rest of the village if there are any manning shortfalls from these meetings but often people will just turn up on spec to contribute to the preparations, despite not having actually put their names down or made it known that they are interested in any particular jobs.

BUNTING

The first real outward sign in the village that Gala Week is on its way is when the bunting goes up. It is almost as if the village is throwing down its marker and demanding that the community commit to the delivery of the event. So it is that an intrepid team of people gather furtively on Top Row one weekday evening early in June, complete with stepladders and could pass as burglars were it not for fact that the bags that they tote do not contain swag but reels of multicoloured ribbon. The best part of the next three hours is then spent liberally distributing the bunting around the village, linking the houses in great chains of red, white and blue, which flutter gently in the breeze. Of course how much pleasure the bunting team derives from the exercise depends on many factors, including the weather, the number of people who turn up for the job and the midges, which can make a test out of even the most pleasant early summer evening. Whatever happens, the cakes that Jill Garmeson cooks up as a reward for the team make the efforts worthwhile.

GALA DAY

On the day of the gala people start moving around the village early (about 11:00am) as there is much to do. For the most part, the preparation work

The children from Litton Church of England Primary School demonstrating the art of May-pole dancing

ahead of the day has gone on over the course of the preceeding weeks but assembly of the event is unrehearsed. It is fortunate that older hands and long-standing residents are around to offer advice and noises of encouragement to the people new to the village. Trestle tables are fetched from various locations and placed in readiness along the course of road in front of the club. Preparations are made on the green for the bouncy castles and coconut shys that are to be held down there. The kettle urn is warmed up in the club kitchen in preparation for the ocean of teas, coffees, cakes and sandwiches that will be demanded and tables and chairs are brought out into the sunshine. The allotted owners of the stalls appear and start to bring together

the accoutrements of their contribution to the day: Plant stall, cake stall, book stall, dice games, tombola, Vera's famous white elephant stall, ice cream, raffle and treasure hunt all line up side-by-side in the sunshine. At 1pm the road is closed off and the traffic

diverted. The crowd and the band gather on the green where they are addressed by the the local vicar Frank Yates, who blesses the well and opens the

Tombola, books, plants - everything must go!

proceedings. The next couple of hours is a throng of people laughing, eating ice cream, meeting old friends and exchanging gossip over a cup of tea and cakes while listening to the band. Wooden balls ricochet off coconuts, balloons escape, chocolate melts and everyone has a good time. As the afternoon wears on people start to drift away until all that is left are the same people who were there at the start of the day, this time picking up litter, folding trestles and dismantling the engines of entertainment for

another year. Exhausted, they drop into garden chairs to enjoy the remainder of the late afternoon sunshine before retiring to the bar to congratulate each other on achieving yet another Gala Day against all the odds.

Following Gala Day, the Well Dressing is left up for a week and attracts many visitors who use the Derbyshire Well Dressings as a good excuse to get out and about in the Peak District to look at the creative offerings of the villages; some grand, some modest. Within the community other events follow on in the next seven days to accompany the Well Dressing and these tend to focus on the club. Quiz nights, pub games, competitions, an evening of games on the green for the kids and general silliness culminate in a party at the club on the Saturday evening, usually entertained by a local act like The Banned. Then, at about 10pm, as it is starting to get dark, everyone assembles on the road outside the club for the torchlight parade; a procession up and down (or

Brian Bingham conducting the band outside the club on Gala Day

should that be down and up) Middle Row with torches, white hankies and accompanied by members of the band who play a jig. The energy of the party and a modicum of alcohol is usually enough to get all but the most taciturn tapping their feet to the beat if not bobbing and weaving like the best-drilled team of Morissers.

Well Dressing

A traditional, annual event in many Derbyshire villages for many hundreds of years, this is the high-light in Cressbrook's packed social calendar

Ingredients:
Wooden frames
Recycled clay
New clay and more water
Old bath for mixing
Feet - with or without welly boots
Builders floats
Black peppercorns
Flower petals - home grown and purchased
Dried camomile, grasses, etc

Tea, coffee, wine
Mosquito spray
Strong helpers to lift the finished wells

Time:
A few weeks to design
1 week to soak boards
1 weekend to mix and tread the clay then as much time over the next five days for petalling, when everyone is welcome, beginners and experts.

Well-dressing has its roots in pagan Earth worship, thanking the spirits of the Earth for the gift of water delivered through the magical portal of the spring. The Romans were known to have conducted such worships and it is likely that the Celts had a similar practice for the tradition to have survived to the present day. The theme of worship was adapted at some point to accommodate the Christian faith and could also have been a Roman influence. In recent times the celebratory side of the event has grown to match its religious significance and Cressbrook is not alone in choosing the village well-dressing as the centerpiece of the annual celebrations.

1 The first stage of Well Dressing in Cressbrook takes place shortly after the New Year when the person presently tasked with the design of the wells, Heidi Savery, starts working on potential designs for this year's wells. This is followed by a meeting at Easter time of the Community Association where the designs of the wells are discussed and approved. Gala happens on the second weekend of June so the Community Association have most of April and May to translate the design for the well into the real thing.

2 The next stage often doesn't happen until late May at which point the wooden frames which hold the well dressing designs are fetched out of storage along with the clay that will hold the design into the frame. The frames and clay are taken to Trinity House where for many years the actual business of putting the well-dressings together has taken place.

3 The frames are laid out and given a good long soaking over a period of several days. The reason for this is to stop the dampness of the clay being taken up by the wood of the frame, drying it out prematurely. Building the well-dressing design on a damp frame can significantly prolong its life.

4 While the frame is soaking, the clay is 'puddled'. Clay that has been rescued from last years design is dumped into an old bath and is supplemented with some new clay to replace any that has been lost or is now too old to use. All of the clay is mashed up together in the bath with water to get it to a smooth consistency.

The best tool for puddling clay is feet, either wellington boot clad or naked. Adults are allowed but have to get in the queue after the kids.

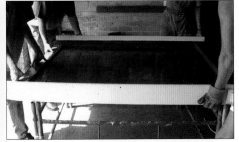

5 The soaked boards are taken into the garage at Trinity House and laid out on trestles.

6 The puddled clay is then carefully applied to the boards by Ken Munns and other willing and able helpers and smoothed out using a builder's float. This gives an even, regular surface on which to work.

7 The next stage is to transfer the design for the well onto the clay surface. This is done by first carefully scribing the design lightly into the surface of the clay and then 'picking out' the lines using peppercorns, which are pushed lightly into the surface.

8 The remainder of the time before Gala is spent filling in the design using a variety of natural materials of appropriate colour. The traditional name for this process is 'Petalling' as often petals or blooms are used to create the colours in the design but it is just as likely that other materials

such as bark, slate chips, camomile and coal will be used where their colours are appropriate.

9 Despite the fact that there never seems to be enough time to create the Well Dressing it always seems to get finished (just!) for Gala Day and on the

morning of the event the boards are carried to the village green and assembled, strapped to a pair of strong metal posts that were put in place many years ago just for that purpose.

Cressbrook always takes photographs of the wells it creates and pictures of wells gone by are displayed around the walls of the club.

115

Thoroughly modern mill

Reconstruction and restoration of the mill was the only option if the buildings were to be saved. David Holmes took up the challenge

Cressbrook Mills ceased operating in 1965 and despite being listed as Grade II* failed to attract any interest as a going concern for many years, to the extent that the effects of time and the weather threatened to undo its fabric for good. It passed through several ownerships until in 1973 it was taken on by David Holmes. At the time Mr Holmes operated a building business from his home in Over Haddon and was finding his existing premises too small for his needs. Following an advertisement in the local press for the site at Cressbrook he acquired the mill and transferred his business from Over Haddon. Initial structural inspections found that most of the buildings on the site were in an advanced state of disrepair. Wye Mill was in the best condition but it was no more than five years away from the onset of structural failure. Rain that had leaked through the roof had already caused rot, which had attacked many of the internal timbers. The roof was made

secure along with the structurally unsound parts of the main buildings while occasionally running repairs were made on the worst affected buildings as and when they were needed. The National Park Authority in the meantime applied pressure to secure the long-term future of this historically significant site.
This situation persisted for several years until trading difficulties experienced by the whole of the construction industry in the late 1980s forced action upon everyone. Mr Holmes had been operating a stone cutting business at the site for a

The Bobbin Mill before restoration

number of years; buying, developing and selling Stancliffe Quarry gritstone. This had proved to be lucrative so when the construction trade dried up he found himself with a large asset and a reasonable amount of capital. At this point there was no obvious viable commercial use for the site and these doubts remained until the early 1990s when the first of the recent wave of housing booms hit the area, at which point it became clear that the mill's

best and probably only long-term prospects lay in their conversion to flats. The proposal was acceptable to the National Park Authorities and permission for the plan was granted. The early stages of the conversion involved the removal of unsafe and non-essential outbuildings, many of which had been added to the main structure of the mill in the years subsequent to its construction by the Phillipses. Once these had been cleared it was possible to proceed with remedial and reconstruction work that the remaining mill buildings needed to make them conform to modern building regulations. It was at this point that significant difficulties were encountered. Investigations showed that while the foundations of Wye Mill were built onto solid bedrock, the foundations of Arkwright's Mill and Cressbrook Mill were structurally unsound, consisting of little more than loose rock and tufa and were completely unsuited to support the intended and agreed purposes of the building. A situation that nothing but major reconstruction work could rectify. Controversially, if the buildings were to exist in perpetuity at the site in a safe state then there was no option but to rebuild them from the foundations up. Once this difficult decision had been made the way was open for the renovation. The smaller units of the Engineering Shed, Cressbrook Mill (renamed during Matthew Dickie's time to the Bobbin Mill) and Arkwright's Mill were

converted first and the funds generated by the sale of the flats in these buildings were rolled forward into the challenging conversion of Wye Mill, which presented its own unique set of problems. Wye Mill's years of neglect had left it with poor internal structural integrity. This was overcome by using the same techniques with which modern tall buildings are built, where poured internal reinforced concrete walls and columns provide the required structural strength and transfer the load away from the curtain walls of the building to the core.

This meant that it was possible to proceed with the internal conversion of the mill with little or no alteration the external fabric. The characteristic and very attractive Georgian look to the building was thus preserved.

Mr Holmes always intended to retain as many original features at the site as was possible within the limits of the requirements of Building Regulations and Listed Building consent. He took great pleasure in particular in preserving the mill race area at the western end of the building, including Matthew Dickie's turbine and the goyt built for Wye Mill by William Newton. The northern wall of the mill race itself is perhaps the oldest remaining structure on the site having probably been built by Richard Arkwright snr some time around 1780. The restoration works also threw up some very interesting discoveries including possibly Arkwright's original goyt from the Cress Brook, which had been hidden in the foundations of Wye Mill as well as the remains of some very old cottages along the side of the river gorge, just below William Newton's dam. These may have been Arkwright's original cottages and the place where William Newton snr first lived and from where he attempted to save the mill from the fire on the night of 15th November 1785. Also important was the creation of an underground car park big enough to accommodate the needs of all of the flats in the mills. Without the clutter of cars around it, the beauty of the original buildings stand out in splendid isolation in the commanding position at the head of the valley that the mill has enjoyed for nearly 200 years. Those areas around the mills where outbuildings have been removed have been carefully landscaped and as the planting matures it is gradually hiding the cold, hard edges of industry and creating instead the soft comfort of residence.

The enthusiastic take-up of the flats in the converted mills by incoming owners has justified all of the difficult decisions that were involved in the restoration of the site. Without prompt action the mills will have without doubt been lost. In making the compromises necessary the site has been saved and is probably now safe for another 200 years at least.

Jim Grindley and Mick Daulton spent six weeks building the dry-stone wall on the path going to Water-cum-Jolly. Using 84 tons of typical Derbyshire stone, the wall is two feet wide at the bottom, tapering to one foot at the top with 'throughs' at the bottom and halfway up to strengthen it, even though there are no sheep or cows in the vicinity to rub on the stones and push the wall down.

117

top: A kingfisher

middle: Lords and Ladies

left: The bridge crossing the weir over the River Wye at Water-cum-Jolly

Flora and fauna and tourists

The diversity of Cressbrook's geological and natural surround ensures that visitors can appreciate the village from both scientific and purely recreational viewpoints

Photograph courtesy of Picture The Past

The mill pool on the Cress Brook

For the residents of Cressbrook, the simple act of either opening a door or glancing though a window confirms to them that they live in a unique and beautiful place. Every view offered by every house in the village is filled with the verdant luxury and the drama of its position while the diversity of life that resides within the scenery emphasises that the beauty of the place is far from just skin deep. This diversity is a product of a coincidence of factors that have combined to create something that is both special and fragile.

GEOGRAPHY

Cressbrook is located in the centre of the limestone uplands that form the White Peak area of the Peak District National Park. The area provides a tremendous range of habitats, which in turn leads to enormous diversity in both plant life and animal life. It is little surprise that Cressbrook is surrounded on all sides by Sites of Special Scientific Interest (SSSIs) and is a part of the wider area of the Wye Valley SSSI.

A major force in local habitat creation in the White Peak are the rivers that flow through the area. The steep-sided valleys that the rivers and their tributaries have created combine with the local climate with incredibly diverse results. Above the valleys the plateau areas are dominated by well-drained grasslands, which have been grazed by animals for many tens of thousands of years and while the limestone rock underneath the grasslands is alkaline, the soil on which they grow is acidic. This is because it is formed from a wind-blown loess that was deposited over the whole area some time soon after the end of the last ice-age. Much of the farmland has been improved through addition of lime but toward the edges of these areas and in unimproved parts much of acidic soil remains. The grasslands thus supports both alkaline loving plants and acid loving as well as tolerant and neutral plants.

Moving down onto the sides of the valleys the habitat changes to well-drained and quite poor soils and screes that support a very wide range of tree species. The soils on the valley floors meanwhile are richly organic and damp and support large numbers of plant species that prefer these conditions. The picture is further complicated by the orientation of the valleys themselves, which over the expanse of the entire upland area offer all possible alignments to the sun and to the prevailing weather. Those slopes that are south facing are significantly warmer and experience far more direct sunlight than those that are north facing. Slopes of a similar pitch and soil type will support significantly different habitats depending on their orientation. Because of this the peak is home to a much greater diversity of plants and animals than would be seen in a flat landscape.

FLORA

The specification for the Cressbrook Dale National Nature Reserve written by English Nature describes the plant life as follows;

"Cressbrook Dale is a steep-sided dale running in a north-south direction

119

containing some spectacular limestone cliffs. The tree canopy is of Ash with a little Wych Elm and a dense shrub layer of Bird-cherry, Field Maple, Guelder Rose, Hazel and Dogwood. The field layer is dominated by Dog's Mercury with patches of Ramsons and Lily-of-the-valley. In a few localities Mezereon and Spurge Laurel occur. It has been suggested that the presence of Small-leaved Lime together with Lily-of-the-valley, Bird-cherry and Dogwood indicates that at least a part of the woodland may be primary .(1) Some extensive areas of scrub occur. On west facing slopes there are areas of 'retrogressive scrub' (2) rich in species such as Dark Red Helleborine, Broad-leaved Helleborine and Bloody Cranesbill. Other areas of scrub are

PAT KELLY

Spring was wonderful. Walking down the hill to school I discovered at least three blue-tits nests in the dry-stone wall. I could pull a stone out and look at all the babay birds, then carefully put the stone back. The woods were full of wild garlic and masses of lily-of-the-valley - I remember all the wonderful smells so well.

Peter, my cousin, used to poach trout and bring them home for Tay. He used to wade into the trout pool and tickle them on their stomachs, then he would grab them and bring them home.

Cowslips and Early Purple orchids, to be seen in spring in Cressbrook Dale and along the Monsal Trail

dominated by Hawthorn with abundant Blackthorn, Rose and Buckthorn. These areas of scrub form a mosaic with tall ungrazed grassland and are very important to insects.

The range of limestone grasslands in this dale is perhaps the finest in the whole of the White Peak. Wardlow Hay Cop, above the Dale, is one of the best outside the dales. It is covered with Meadow Oat and Carnation Sedge and areas of acidic grassland dominated by Mat Grass. Stemless Thistle occurs here at one of its most northerly sites in Britain. In the dale, Heath False-brome, another species near its northern limit also occurs. On very poor soils below the crags are found the rare Bird's-foot Sedge and

Fingered sedge. In many parts of the dale the grasslands are remarkable for the richness of limestone plant communities and for the insects that they support. There are a number of mine spoil heaps in the dale where Spring Sandwort is common and Rock Hutchinsia abundant. Both species are particularly associated with such sites but scarce elsewhere in the country. Cressbrook Dale is one of the most important sites in the region for lichens growing on limestone and in the moister parts of the Dale there is a rich Bryophyte flora."

Ownership of the Frith passed to The Stanton Estate Company when Matthew Dickie Ltd went into liquidation in 1938. Up until then certain parts of it were coppiced for firewood and building materials, particularly hazel. Since 1938 however, beyond periods of essential maintenance the land has been left more or less undisturbed. This has undoubtedly contributed significantly to the abundance and variety of plant life on show in the Dale.

1 Woodland that was established after the last ice age and that has remained essentially unchanged since.
2 Scrub that grazing by animals has prevented from developing freely

BIRDLIFE

The richness and variety of a local invertebrate community is a key factor in the creation of diversity higher up the food chain among the predator species. The variety of invertebrate life in Cressbrook Dale is very impressive and is supported by the amount of dead and decaying vegetable matter in the underbrush of the Frith, which is littered with fallen trees and is home to innumerable species of insect. Bird watching in Cressbrook, therefore, is highly rewarding. While it is possible to just sit in the garden and tick off the species as they visit the bird table, venturing just a short way into the surrounding fields and woods can double the number of species observed. In addition to the regular visitors to the garden that will be familiar to bird watchers anywhere, Cressbrook gardens are also home to Bullfinch, Goldfinch, Willow Tit, Long-tailed Tit, Greater Spotted Woodpecker, Treecreeper and Nuthatch while the chack-chack of the local Jackdaw clan offers a constant and somewhat notorious background conversation. Just away from the places where people go in Cressbrook but still to be seen if you look carefully enough, are birds such as Jay, Green Woodpecker, Mistle Thrush, Goldcrest, Wheatear and Sparrowhawk while present but only seen occasionally and keeping themselves away from people, are Flycatchers, Ravens, Buzzards,

Ravensdale Crag in Cressbrook Dale is named after the ravens who live there

A nesting Peregrine and chicks

Gosshawk and Peregrine Falcon. Nightly entertainment is given freely by the large and very vocal local population of Tawny Owls while the Barn Owl can also be seen occasionally. Down on the river Wye, along with the usual wildfowl suspects, there are also Dippers, Kingfisher, Grey Wagtails and Dabchicks.

FAUNA

Curiously, one of the more common countryside beasts, the fox, is not a frequent visitor to the bins of houses in Cressbrook. That position is reserved for badgers and local people have learnt that inattention to the secure fixing of the lid on a bin will result in the generous redistribution of its contents by curious brocks. Many a good-intentioned holidaymaker has had their careful and considerate placement of waste in preparation for the following days collection undone in this manner. Just on the outside of the village a lucky individual may spot one of the local weasels and on a walk along the River Wye, through Water-cum-Jolly to Litton Mill an attentive observer may see a Water Vole. Even more rarely, but still present nonetheless, is the very occasional Stoat which can be seen on the Monsal Trail. Benefiting from same rich variety in insect life that attracts birds in the area, are a number of different species of bat, including pipistrelles.

TOURISM

The Peak District has long been a place where people come to relax. The area around Cressbrook is something of a jewel in the crown in this respect and has been a sought after destination for visitors for many years. The collapsed gorge of Water-

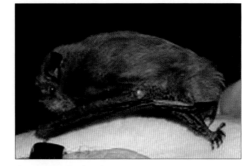

A pipistrelle bat

cum-Jolly Dale offers those who follow the path through it to Litton Mill a unique and beautiful perspective on the effects of energetic rivers on limestone landscapes while its cliffs offer endless possibilities to rock climbers. Around the corner the tranquillity of the ancient woodland of the Frith provides limitless potential to students of nature of all ages and a dramatic counterpoint to the close-cropped and denuded landscape of the dale immediately to the north, below the 'Stargate' path to Wardlow Mires, where the winterborn Cress Brook springs in response to the autumn rains. Those less inclined to venture into the landscape on foot can still sample its riches from the comfort of a motor vehicle thanks to William Newton's road, which links the bottom of Monsal Dale to the road to Litton high above it via an outrageous hairpin bend buried deep in the trees of the Frith.

D's Brewstop - 'tea, coffee, soup, ice-creams and eat your own sarnies' - is run by Dave Teare and is a popular stop with walkers at the weekend,, en route to Water-cum-Jolly

Rubicon Wall at Water-cum-Jolly popular with climbers all year round

A winters tale

Because of its situation, a harsh winter can almost bring Cressbrook to a halt. Here residents describe amazing incidents from the worst winters

Tansley Dale

MRS DAYKIN

I remember once, this was soon after I came and I travelled from Taddington. I managed to get to Monsal Head, it was so bad and so slippery and icy, so I sat down and slid down. Partway down there was a big van I tried to cling on to, but I couldn't it was so icy. Anyway, eventually I got to the bottom. We carried on for the day for those who turned up - there wouldn't be many - and Martin from the farm took me back on the tractor at night, so I gaily stood there on the back of the tractor, Queen of Sheba you know. I've had some slippery and scary times coming here. When I lived in Buxton and coming round Millers Dale it was dreadful, then from Litton to Cressbrook was a nightmare. The only reason I was looking forward to retiring was because of these bad winters and then as soon as I retired the winters improved. The playground being on such a slope is lethal when it's icy and I know once, not long before I retired, it seemed to clear up by lunchtime you know and I'd forgotten all about it. The boys were playing football and I was kicking it with them then suddenly there I was down on the floor. I broke my wrist and I ended up at Chesterfield hospital. There must have been a little ice left on the slope. We had the garden after Mr Worsencroft gave it up as a garden and the children brought in their sledges and it was lovely out there. The milk would arrive for the children in $1/3$ pint bottles and we used to put them on the warm pipes to defrost.

PAT KELLY

That winter was one of the worst ever for snow in the Peak District. We were off school for a month - Mrs Brett who usually cycled from Tideswell couldn't get to Cressbrook. We were completely cut off. The snow was up to the bedroom windows at the cottage and we got to the front door through a tunnel of frozen snow - Mrs Lomas's son from Litton had dug us out. We children had a wonderful magic winter - it was like the alps - a winter wonderland with deep frozen drifts and we skated and sledged all winter. We had to go in convoy to Tideswell twice a week for groceries, one of the villagers led us, walking on the tops of the dry-stone walls which were covered in snow, pulling our sledges heaped with produce. When the thaw came we reluctantly went back to school. The hill down was wonderful to sledge on and the village kids used to pile their sledges with snowballs and pelt the poor London evacuees when they came out of the Lodge gates on their way to school.

AUBREY HOWE

The winters are improving. Then the roads going on the top could be blocked for days you know. I was only small but there is a photograph where they stood on the snow touching the top of the telegraph poles. In the winter I used to have to take milk every year and meet the tanker at Wardlow Mires or even Litton sometimes because of the snow; and I remember one year I took it for nine weeks. Yes, I used to pump it out of the tanks and into another emergency tank and meet the tanker 'cos it couldn't get anywhere near us.

I mean to be honest with you the thing was they hadn't got the machinery in those days to move it 'cos as fast as you dug little paths through, the snow just blew straight back and it all filled in again.

HARRIET ALLEN

Our two horses, we'd got the two then Queenie and Star, and Matt used to like them kept outside. He said they were better outside. He used to feed them of course but the snow got very bad and so one morning I was lying in bed and I said to Matt 'I'm sure I've heard Star whinnying' and of course you could slide those windows across couldn't you at the farm, so I got out of bed and I went to the window and there she was coming down the yard and Queenie was coming with her, following her. Matt got his trousers on right quick and I got in the window bottom and I sat talking to her. Well they'd walked over the wall when they were in that field down the dale, the snow was so high that they walked over the wall. So of course then they went into the stables and they stopped there 'til weather improved.

I know another winter when we had a terrific snow. We had a post office in the village, we did have a shop as I say but the post office used to sell bread and groceries and Mr Thorpe that lived there, he came to my husband and asked if there was any chance of fetching some groceries from the station because he'd ordered some bread and different stuff and couldnt get there. So my husband said he'd try and get the sledge out which he'd made, this was so that he could take the hay up to a small barn which we rented up at Leisure Farm where we had some cows. So he used Star, she was the chief horse not Queenie - I don't know whether we'd still got her then. We got rid of her, she were bad tempered and she'd bite anybody but Star you could trust her. Off they went and they fetched the groceries from Monsal Dale station for Mr Thorpe. It was you know, really deep snow and anyway he managed it and he took all the groceries back up to the top of the village for Mr Thorpe.

Dark Lane in the snow

Middle Row, waiting for the snow to melt before venturing out

New Houses, an exposed location on the road from Cressbrook to Litton

123

References used in this book

Web sources

Local Heritage Initiative	www.lhi.org.uk
Economic History Services	www.eh.net
Access to Archives	www.a2a.org.uk
Peak District National Park	www.peakdistrict.org
Picture The Past	www.picturethepast.org.uk
Manchester Archives	www.manchester.gov.uk/libraries
Westminster Archives	www.westminster.gov.uk/libraries/
English Nature	www.english-nature.org.uk
English Heritage	www.english-heritage.org.uk
Stockport Local Heritage Library	www.stockport.gov.uk
Derbyshire Local Studies Library	www.derbyshire.gov.uk
East Midlands Oral History Archive	www.le.ac.uk/emoha
Jean Stone's genealogy research	www.cressbrook.com/citydesk/
Cressbrook Club	www.cressbrookclub.org.uk

Printed Sources

McConnel, J W	A Century of Fine Cotton Spinning
Adam, W	Gem of the Peak
Allen, M	Cressbrook
Bray, W	A Sketch of a Tour into Derbyshire and Yorkshire
Gloag, J	Mr Loudon's England
Frow, E & F (ed)	Dark Satanic Mills, Child Apprentices in Derbyshire Spinning Factories
Hudson, W	Through Limestone Hills
Lee, C H	A Cotton Enterprise, 1795-1840, A history of McConnel & Kennedy, Fine Cotton Spinners
Mackenzie, M	Cressbrook and Litton Mills, 1779-1835. Part 1, DAJ, vol. 88
Mackenzie, M	Cressbrook Mill, 1810-1835, DAJ, vol. 90
Morris, C (ed)	The Journeys of Celia Feinnes
Thompson, P	The Voice of the Past
Ternant, D	Cressbrook Mill, The Journal of Industrial Archeology (part)
Sheldon, E	Notes on Cressbrook, Derbyshire
Unsworth, W	Portrait of the River Derwent

To Jeff, Jane, Mike and Helena,
Many thanks for your support and
patience while we produced this book

In memory of Arthur Barnes who shared
his personal memories of Cressbrook with us.
21st May 1925 - 13th September 2005

Carole Perks, Chris Gilbert and Hilary Stephens, November 2005